THE CONTEST FOR THE INDIAN OCEAN

THE CONTEST FOR THE INDIAN OCEAN

And the Making of a New World Order

DARSHANA M. BARUAH

YALE UNIVERSITY PRESS
NEW HAVEN AND LONDON

For information about this and other Yale University Press publications, please contact:
U.S. Office: sales.press@yale.edu   yalebooks.com
Europe Office: sales@yaleup.co.uk   yalebooks.co.uk

Set in Minion Pro by IDSUK (DataConnection) Ltd
Printed in Great Britain by Clays Ltd, Elcograf S.p.A

Library of Congress Control Number: 2024939684

ISBN 978-0-300-27091-4

A catalogue record for this book is available from the British Library.

10 9 8 7 6 5 4 3 2 1

To Ma and Deta

Contents

Maps, Figures, and Tables

Maps

Maps 1, 3, and 4 redrawn from Carnegie sample maps

Figures

Tables

Abbreviations

ANC	Andaman and Nicobar Command
ANI	Andaman and Nicobar Islands
ASW	Anti-submarine warfare
BIOT	British Indian Ocean Territory
BRI	Belt and Road Initiative
DOWA	Deep Ocean Water Application
EEZs	Exclusive Economic Zones
EIA	(US) Energy Information Administration
EU	European Union
ICJ	International Court of Justice
IJN	Imperial Japanese Navy
IOC	Indian Ocean Commission
IORA	Indian Ocean Rim Association
ISR	Intelligence, Surveillance, and Reconnaissance
IUU	Illegal, Unidentified, and Unregulated (fishing)
JCS	Joint Chiefs of Staff
MDA	Maritime Domain Awareness
MSR	Maritime Silk Road
NSSM	National Security Study Memorandums
PLA	People's Liberation Army

ABBREVIATIONS

PRC   People's Republic of China
RMIFC   Regional Maritime Information Fusion Centre
SAARC   South Asian Association for Regional Cooperation
SIDS   Small Island Developing States
SLOCs   Sea lanes of communications
UAE   United Arab Emirates
UDA   Underwater Domain Awareness
UN   United Nations
US   United States
USSR   Union of Soviet Socialist Republics

Acknowledgments

This acknowledgments section was the final piece I wrote for this book but a very important one. Like most authors, I am deeply grateful to many people in my personal and professional life who have been instrumental in completing this book. My gratitude goes beyond the time I actively worked on the book to include those who made it possible for me to be in the position to be able to write a book in the first place.

In my professional life, there is no one to whom I am more indebted than Dr. C. Raja Mohan. CRM, as I refer to him, is and has been my most important mentor. I had the opportunity to begin my career with him as his intern in 2013, and learned some of the most important and useful professional lessons in the six years that I worked with him.

I have had the good fortune of finding strong support for my research and ideas throughout my career. This support has come from people whom I look up to and hold in high regard. I feel fortunate to have had their interest in my work. In particular I want to recognize the support of Junko Chano (Sasakawa Peace Foundation), Rory Medcalf (Australian National University), and Ashley J. Tellis (Carnegie Endowment for International Peace). Chano-san has been instrumental, as she supported my idea of undertaking research for this book in Tokyo. She created and gave me the space to contemplate and research concepts which underpin this book. My deepest gratitude goes to Rory Medcalf and Ashley J. Tellis, who over the years have again supported my ideas and invited me into important rooms and conversations. I am grateful for their guidance during many times in my career and as I moved through think tanks in different countries building on this research.

A harsh truth about this profession and this research is that most work on maritime security or international security more generally is written, led, and shaped by men. At times the lack of women in this space or the lack of space for women scholars has been crushingly discouraging. Amidst this, however, I want to recognize the help from individuals in the navies of the Indo-Pacific. I have had the opportunity to work with those of India, the US, France, Australia, Japan, Sri Lanka, the Maldives, and Singapore, among others. Despite almost always being in rooms full of men, these were the spaces in which I was most comfortable sharing, expressing, and debating my ideas and thoughts on maritime security. Many officers from these services, some of whom are now my friends, welcomed and supported me and gave me the opportunity to speak to decision-makers and senior leaders. These conversations and opportunities to brainstorm ideas have been crucial in my understanding of maritime security and the maritime domain. At a personal level, I have deep admiration for the intellectual and welcoming approach of many of the naval officers I have encountered. Thank you for viewing me as your equal while I often juggled justifying my presence in other rooms because of my gender, age, and the color of my skin.

I could not write a book without acknowledging Assam and the Assamese in me. The endeavor for this book is also an ode to Hukanpukhuri (Sukanpukhuri), my dear home in Assam—the place I love so much and value more than any other. Alongside this is an acknowledgment to my Aju Koka (great grandfather), Durga Prasad

Mozinder Baruah, an Assamese poet and playwright. He was a literary giant in Assam and his work is still taught and read in the region. I read his work in Assamese while writing this book, in moments of stagnation and confusion. This is a small ode both to koka and to Assam. It is my hope that through this book, I will also have put Assam on readers' minds, in whatever small way possible.

My intention of mentioning Assam is not just to add a personal story but to highlight my region and the geographical space I come from. Even those most familiar with India are unfamiliar with its northeast. Much like the maritime discourse in subcontinental discussions, I found my culture, history, heritage, food, and even Assam's existence missing from conversations about India, both in South Asia and at an international level. I will not go into the political and historical sensitivities regarding my homeland, but I acutely understand the importance of geography and what it means to be sitting at the crossroads of competing powers' interests. I grew up in the midst of it; I lived the turmoil, and it has had an immense impact on me in searching for the smaller and more nuanced details in understanding how geography impacts the roles of players.

To my parents, Anima and Binoy: thank you for being so sure of yourselves and so confident in the people you are. I have the deepest admiration toward my parents for dreaming of a world they hadn't seen themselves. For supporting my every idea, even if they didn't understand it, including moving to and living in countries and places they have never seen or experienced. I could not be more grateful and lucky to have them as the two people who have fundamentally shaped the person I am today. To my sister, Liza, thank you for stepping up and encouraging me to go down roads when Ma and Deta could not envision further. Thank you for always speaking up for me and standing by my side.

As this book began the process of going to proofs, I undertook the process of moving continents. It threw me into a whirlpool of immigration chaos, legal haze, uncertainties, and deep exhaustion. I could not have gotten through much of it if not for my brilliant, compassionate, inspiring, and selfless friends—from Assam to the wider world. The most remarkable moments of my time in DC were about discovering strong, inspiring, supportive, and absolutely encouraging female friendships. I must say, moving from Delhi to Tokyo to Washington, DC, and now to Sydney, I have been carried, loved, and supported by incredible friends who continue to give me strength to explore, find, and live in communities and countries where I have no family or history. I feel incredibly fortunate to have met and become friends with such remarkable people and I could not have juggled my life, writing this book, a full-time job, and post-pandemic woes without the support and love I received from these friendships. There is a lot I have to thank you all for—you know who you are, and you are so dear to me.

Joanna Godfrey, my editor at Yale, is remarkable and I have been so fortunate to develop this book and work on it with her. My initial proposal was to write a book focused entirely on the role of islands in shaping great power competition. Conversations with Joanna made me realize the value and need for a book discussing the importance of the Indian Ocean first and the island story within. My gratitude goes to Joanna and colleagues at Yale for all the support and help in finalizing the manuscript. Thank you to Yale's production team, particularly Rachael Lonsdale and Meg Pettit, who have been patient with me as I juggled my competing priorities and deadlines for this book and paperwork for Australia simultaneously. My special thanks also to colleagues and friends at the Carnegie Endowment for support and understanding as I wrote this book while building the Indian Ocean Initiative and its projects—in particular, colleagues at the library, the program coordinator, and Junior Fellows at the South Asia and Asia Program. Deep gratitude to Evan A. Feigenbaum for encouraging me to build a new program at Carnegie and helping me realize the vision for it—I could not have produced an annual Islands Dialogue, an interactive map, the various projects, and indeed this book without your support. I would also like to acknowledge Carnegie's incredible communications team who have all been so very supportive.

Special thanks to Reica Shimozawa and Rhea Menon for excellent research support through different stages of conceptualizing and finalizing this manuscript. Reica was instrumental in providing research support toward Japanese archival documents I have used for this book from the *Senshi Soshu* series.

This is my first book and I have no doubt there will be many mistakes and oversights. They are all mine and I fully accept them. My aim is to contribute to debates around maritime security and the Indian Ocean: I hope that this book can energize these important discussions and debate the path forward.

With gratitude.

Washington, DC
May 2024

Preface

Maritime security has always been an aspect of great power competition fascinating to me. Almost all major conflicts have a maritime component—and military victory on a large scale certainly involves and requires a naval victory. Take, for example, World War II, in which the decisive battle played out across the Pacific with the attack on Hawaii and the capture of Okinawa; the ocean space between these two islands and the control of communications lines between them have been a source of study for all navies and maritime powers since. More broadly, we need not elaborate on the naval expeditions of imperial France, England, Portugal, and the Netherlands (among other European nations) and their impact on establishing these empires as global powers in the first place. Control and surrender of the seas and oceans have always been instrumental in any country's global power ambitions. The impact of the seas on the global economy, from international trade to food and resources, only reinforced the importance of the domain in my mind. As a student of history, the significance of the maritime domain for powers in past periods of regional and global conflict further underlined the continued and increasing importance of maritime security on competition and conflict, even under different security structures and frameworks.

The implications of sea power, sea lanes of communications, and their interlinkages with twenty-first-century geopolitics in understanding the affairs of the world and great power competition were already obvious to me. That the concerns surrounding the artificial islands in the South China Sea were more than a regional conflict, and were in fact a marker for twenty-first-century global maritime security, became clear as I undertook research and writing on maritime security. The key phenomenon which was different, or rather new, for me, was that maritime security in the twenty-first century was becoming an important pillar of foreign policy engagements in a way the world hadn't witnessed since the two world wars.

This book is very much a product of my research, conversations, and writing on maritime security over the last decade. I wanted to emphasize how maritime security was and is becoming a key aspect of foreign policy engagements. The more I tried to build that into my research, the more I understood the disconnect between maritime security and foreign policy. Yet the pivot to the Indo-Pacific is one of the most defining shifts in geopolitical conversation today—a new theater of geopolitical competition across the oceans. Such a conversation is increasingly urgent—indeed, we should have made a point of understanding and learning about maritime security and its implications for foreign policy several years ago.

I have had the opportunity to live and work in different maritime capitals including Delhi, Tokyo, Canberra, and Washington, DC. These experiences have been further accentuated by engagements, collaborations, and conversations with officials and scholars in France, the United Kingdom, Singapore, Indonesia, the Maldives, Fiji, Sri Lanka, and Mauritius, among others. Following the thread of maritime security across the Indo-Pacific I found it fascinating how the views on what actually constitutes maritime security differed significantly among the many players. It differed even among partners and allies discussing strategies and approaches to the same problem. This book has been shaped by the many different views and perspectives from the various capitals which I have witnessed. Within these conversations, I felt, the Indian Ocean was the least understood, the least studied, and the least reflected upon region, despite the fact that it is a theater which provides a bridge in understanding the many pillars of Indo-Pacific and maritime security.

An important part of my research is my work on island nations and the role they play in shaping geopolitical competition. I truly do think that the choices made by island nations in the Indian Ocean will greatly come to shape how we understand and study the maritime domain. This book is a dedicated effort to break away from the continental silo of the Indian Ocean—or as I like to frame it, the continentalization of a maritime domain—and to reconceptualize the ocean as one theater. That is, to hold a true maritime approach.

This book is not about one or two players, nor about competition between two superpowers. It is about maritime security in the Indian Ocean and the many players who shape the regional dynamics today. In that, a central focus is in addressing the close alliance between maritime security and foreign policy in the twenty-first century.

I have spent much of my career working in think tanks primarily in India, Japan, and the US. My experience has enabled me to listen, interact with, and understand how different countries frame, shape, and build responses to their national security concerns. Progressing my career through the ranks of think tanks has often placed me in rooms where I witnessed the creation of ideas, policies, and partnerships. Although think tanks are credited as spaces or incubators for ideas, the greatest advantage for me was to watch from the sidelines and learn how those with power view the world and debate policies. This is somewhere ingrained in my own personal consciousness as well. As someone who was born and raised in Assam (northeast India), at the periphery of decision-making, we watched the powerful in Delhi make decisions about our region, at times disempowered and without consultation. I have always found the voices, thoughts, and perspectives of those who stand on the margins of important conversations insightful. I approached my research on islands in the same way. I watched great powers sometimes talk over island nations while discussing issues and challenges important to them. And so, as I began my own interactions with island nations, it became clear to me where the bigger world powers were missing connections and linkages.

A few caveats and explanations regarding the structure and contents of the book.

There are many stories within the Indian Ocean context, and they deserve their own space and attention. One of the critical stories is that of India's rise and role as an Indian Ocean actor. While I have touched on the India story, this is not a book about India and the Indian Ocean (which deserves a book of its own). Rather, this book looks to understand the Indian Ocean today as a twenty-first-century theater and India as one of the players—an important, but not the only, one. Chapter 2 charts the US history of the Indian Ocean from Washington's perspective because that is less known. There is not much extant literature drawing on US archives on how Washington approached the Indian Ocean during the Cold War; Chapter 2 is dedicated to providing some insights into that while also seeking to better understand how a nation with great power intentions tends to compete in and view the Indian Ocean. Moreover, the competition with China today helps us to understand US history and presence in the region. The work on the underwater domain in Chapter 6 is new. I have identified issues such as undersea cables and deep-sea mining as new areas of competition that have connections and implications for geopolitics and military security. This is very much an ongoing research effort and an area where the conversation is quite nascent. Given there are limited international treaties dedicated to governing and addressing these issues in the underwater domain, it was a significant challenge in writing about them in the book. Nevertheless, closed-door conversations and my understanding of the maritime domain underpin the significance of the underwater domain as the next theater for competition, and I find it necessary to include that in the book, even in a limited capacity. Similarly, I am not an expert on climate change, but I do understand the importance of climate security and its significance to foreign policy choices for island nations, and therefore it also features in the book.

It is my hope and goal that this book will contribute to the literature on maritime security and generate new dialogues on the importance of the Indian Ocean. I hope it holds enough ideas and provokes bold thoughts which will help us understand and shape how maritime security interacts with geopolitics over the next decades.

I have been fortunate enough to write this Preface with a direct view of the Indian Ocean, from the Maldives. Looking at the waves crashing along the shoreline and considering how the ocean has been such an integral part of cultural identity to so many across its expanse, it is my hope that this book will generate new conversations and a new approach to how we think about and engage with the Indian Ocean.

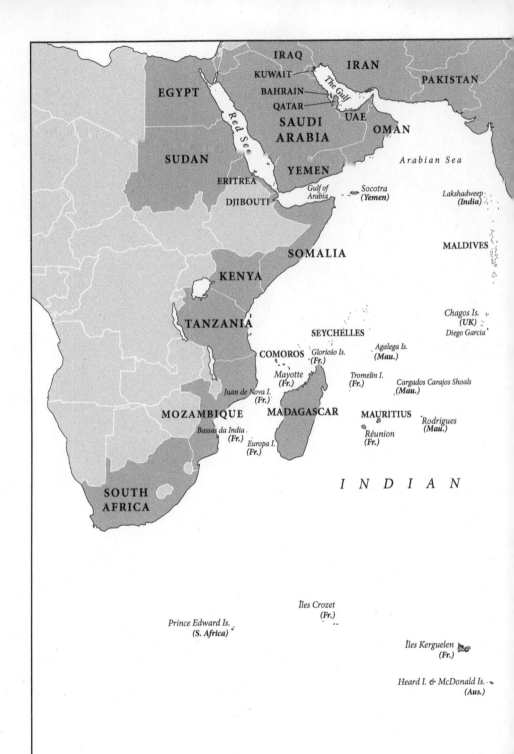

Map 1. The Indian Ocean.

BANGLADESH

NDIA

MYANMAR

Bay of
Bengal

THAILAND

Andaman Is.
(India)

Nicobar Is.
(India)

SRI
LANKA

MALAYSIA

I N D O N E S I A

Christmas I.
(Aus.)

Cocos Is.
(Aus.)

O C E A N

les Amsterdam
les Saint-Paul
(Fr.)

Pacific Ocean

AUSTRALIA

☐ States bordering the Indian Ocean

0   1500 miles

0   1500 km

1

Introduction
Geography and Geopolitics

Throughout history, the Indian Ocean has remained a key theater facilitating the movement of goods and people leading to influences of culture, religion, architecture, literature, and food traveling across the region. These influences today, in the twenty-first century, are seen in the many sub-regions of the Indian Ocean; whether of Portuguese influence in Goa (India), Arab influence in Comoros (Africa), or spices that are common to many Indian Ocean cuisines. Capturing a historical account of the flow of ideas, people, and trade across the ocean, Sugata Bose, in his book *A Hundred Horizons*, notes, "The ocean was—and, in many ways, continues to be— characterized by specialized flows of capital and labor, skills and services, ideas and culture."[1] Bose uses the devastating 2004 Indian Ocean tsunami to remind us of the ripple effects one part of the ocean can create for the entire region. The destructive waves from the tsunami traveled within hours from Indonesia in the east to Somalia in the west. It is a sharp reminder of the geography and its consequences for the people of the area—an ocean that is home to regions, cultures, and markets as diverse as Asia, Africa, and the Middle East. In politics, this very geography has been central in deciding the fate of its people, whether during the European colonization of Asia and Africa or the geopolitics of the Cold War era. In the twenty-first century, it is again the geography of the Indian Ocean that is forcing its sub-regions and its people to the center of geopolitical competition.

Despite the exchange of culture and people through different centuries in the Indian Ocean, however, the region has struggled to create a common identity, in a similar manner to other oceanic littorals, such as the Pacific islands, or Southeast Asia bordering the South China Sea or western Pacific. The Indian Ocean instead is divided by varying religions, cultures, and societies set in continental silos, which diminishes the maritime connectivity between all the nations bordering the ocean. The sheer size of the ocean plays a role in this, but it is also the division of the Indian Ocean into smaller sub-groups, or dominant landmasses, particularly after the Cold War, that has accentuated this tendency.

The diversity of the region poses the biggest challenge in creating a common identity, with varying degrees of differences in politics, governance, society, culture, and economics of the Indian Ocean littorals and its islands. In the post-1945 world, as nations across the Indian Ocean and its rim gained independence from their colonial rulers, countries looked to their continental neighbors with a more domestic focus, working on creating national identities and unifying people within their new borders. Sub-regional groupings provided the format, platform, and support to explore opportunities as well as address common challenges among the newly independent states. Over time, after the Cold War era, the Indian Ocean as one continuous region disappeared into the periphery of geopolitical conversations. Instead of an Indian Ocean community, most littorals found themselves in sub-regional divisions dominated by South Asia, Africa, and the Middle East, with distinct continental challenges and concerns.

So why look at the Indian Ocean today and what is its relevance in the geopolitics of the twenty-first century? The strategic importance of the maritime domain in foreign policy engagements has been accentuated by the Indo-Pacific[2] becoming a new geographic theater that brings together collaborations, interactions, and mutual interests among nations across the Indian and Pacific oceans, and captures the reality of globalization and the movement of goods, people, and supply chains in the twenty-first century. As the Indo-Pacific gained more traction in world affairs, nations across the two oceans began to adopt and craft their own Indo-Pacific policies, exploring new avenues for collaboration and partnership. As a result, maritime security, traditionally a navy-led effort and conversation, has become a core pillar of foreign policy engagements within the Indo-Pacific discourse. This has brought issues of maritime security and developments in the maritime domain back into the geopolitical conversation and great power competition. However, maritime security itself, in the last several decades, has existed in the periphery of geopolitical discourse, and the Indian Ocean is the less examined theater within the Indo-Pacific.

This book argues that the Indian Ocean is the key theater for competition within the Indo-Pacific construct. The geopolitics of the twenty-first century, which has largely taken on a maritime focus, is changing the dynamics in the Indian Ocean. This is primarily driven by two key aspects. First, as the United States and China compete for influence and power across the globe, their competition will be heightened in the Indian Ocean as the central theater, with multiple regional dynamics unfolding simultaneously involving countries such as India, Australia, Japan, and France. As countries around the world have adopted the Indo-Pacific as a new geographical theater, maritime security has come to play a key role in strategic and foreign policy discourses. Second, given this renewed attention to maritime security, island nations—often ignored, but occupying a critical maritime geography—will come to play a significant role in shaping this geopolitical competition. In a new geopolitical environment, as sovereign nations rather than colonial outposts, island nations today are looking to maximize their role, place, and opportunities in the new geopolitical competition of the twenty-first century. They see both an opportunity and a threat in today's geopolitics.

This book aims to explore and highlight the consequences and strategic implications of the Indian Ocean in the emerging geopolitical competition of the twenty-first century. In doing so, the book seeks to draw attention to the role of islands and their significance in the Indian Ocean as the islands navigate complex security partnerships and economic ties with bigger powers. The islands dotting the Indian Ocean—from the Strait of Malacca to the Mozambique Channel—hold key geographic positions with great strategic and military importance. Moreover, these very islands were critical during the European colonization of the region, as well as during World War II, for establishing dominance and control across the vast Indian Ocean. However, today, these islands (with the same geography) have greater agency as independent, sovereign nations (as opposed to being imperial colonies) shaping their own foreign policy, security, and economic choices.

This book seeks to provide an overview of the strategic importance of the Indian Ocean. After the end of World War II, and particularly after the end of the Cold War, as the United States, a Pacific power, took on the role of a dominant global player, the conversations and geopolitics of the Indian Ocean began to be pushed to the periphery of global affairs and broken down into sub-regional dynamics. This book aims to correct the contemporary narrative on the Indian Ocean, underscoring its relevance and importance at a time when the literature and policy conversation are focused on the Pacific. This book and its chapters are an attempt to recognize the Indian Ocean and the role it will play in shaping the Indo-Pacific in years to come.

The book makes three main arguments: that the Indian Ocean constitutes one geographic space; that competition with China will become significant in the Indian Ocean; and that islands' agency will shape great power competition.

The Indian Ocean as one geographic space

Although the Indian Ocean lost its geopolitical importance following the Cold War, its geography is strategically consequential. Most importantly, to understand the implications of the Indian Ocean today, its many players, and evolving dynamics, it is necessary to study and examine the ocean as one continuous geographic space. The study of a maritime domain requires a maritime approach. There is a need to re-study the Indian Ocean from the Red Sea to the Indonesian straits, encompassing the eastern coast of Africa, the Persian Gulf, South Asia, and Australia. It is also important to understand the role of European players such as France—a significant actor with military capabilities and interests in the region. This book, through its chapters, will establish the growing importance of the ocean and its emerging dynamics and trends for geopolitical competition, underpinned by examining the ocean as one continuous space. The following factors capture the importance of viewing the Indian Ocean as one geographic maritime space.

Connectivity

The stability of the Indian Ocean is central for connectivity and trading routes between Asia, Europe, Africa, and the Middle East. Instability or limited conflict in any of the regions would potentially carry significant economic and strategic implications for the wider region, with global implications. An often-cited argument in favor of the Indian Ocean's strategic importance is the presence of crucial sea lanes of communications (SLOCs) and the large energy trade (oil and petroleum) transiting through the region. The United States (US) Energy Information Administration (EIA) identifies seven key chokepoints as "major trade routes for global seaborne oil transportation."[3] The EIA defines chokepoints as "narrow channels along widely used global sea routes for oil transport, with some so narrow that restrictions are placed on the size of the vessel that can navigate through them."[4] Keeping these chokepoints open, stable, and accessible is critical for shipping, energy transportation, and movement of goods and commerce between the major hubs of the world.

Out of the seven critical SLOCs, four are in the Indian Ocean: first, the Strait of Hormuz connecting the Persian Gulf and its littorals to the Indian Ocean; second, the Bab-el-Mandeb connecting the Red Sea to the Indian Ocean through the Gulf of Aden; third, the Strait of Malacca connecting the western Pacific Ocean to the Indian Ocean; and, finally, the Suez Canal connecting the Mediterranean Sea to the Indian Ocean via the Red Sea. Additionally, the Indian Ocean is also home to the Mozambique Channel between Madagascar and Mozambique, a key trade route for the eastern coast of Africa as well as for trade transiting around the Cape of Good Hope to Africa, Europe, and the Middle East. These four chokepoints, along with the Mozambique Channel, border the continental sub-regions of the Middle East, Africa, South Asia, Southeast Asia, and Australia, all connected via the Indian Ocean.

In strategic terms, the ability to protect as well as disrupt these key chokepoints would offer asymmetric advantages during both peacetime and conflict. Access to and influence over the Indian Ocean chokepoints and SLOCs are therefore at the heart of the evolving maritime tussle in the twenty-first century. While competing nations with global ambitions, such as the US and China, seek such power and have the necessary maritime capabilities, they are also far away from these critical SLOCs. Maritime powers historically during the colonial period—under the United Kingdom,[5] Portugal,[6] and France—or, more recently, under the US, Japan, or Germany during World War II,[7] were nations outside of the Indian Ocean that controlled or aimed to control the SLOCs to further their own strategic interests. Therefore, these powers' presence, control, dominance, and influence over the region played a defining role in shaping Indian Ocean history. Between the two world wars, colonization of key islands and littorals for use as way stations was succeeded by the use of naval bases and military facilities, allowing extra-regional powers to establish a presence. These bases, more importantly, allowed distant navies to sustain their presence in maritime theaters far from the coastal shorelines. Chapter 3 discusses the importance of chokepoints, geography, and the Indian Ocean in further detail.

While the security environment today is significantly different from those of the Cold War or World War II periods, the ability to maintain a presence near, or have access to, strategic chokepoints remains central to nations' maritime strategies. Today, we witness a similar desire to establish and sustain maritime presence in distant waters with the rise of China and its global and maritime ambitions. Resident powers, such as India, with a critical geography in the Indian Ocean, also play an important role. Traditionally categorized as way stations in naval campaigns, the islands of the Indian Ocean today are emerging to become significant players in the new game, creating a critical difference for understanding of great power competition in the maritime domain. While India, the US, and China compete to gain or maintain their strategic advantages, the islands of the Indian Ocean lie closest to these chokepoints and SLOCs important to those nations and their friends and partners. From Sri Lanka to Madagascar, these islands oversee the main entry and exit points to and from the Indian Ocean. In combination with the island territories from Cocos (Keeling) in the east to Socotra in the west, this creates an island chain, allowing for disruptions or domination of the Indian Ocean. Despite their critical geography in the Indian Ocean throughout history, colonization, and the island nations' limited capability and access to the great powers, reduced their agency and influence during the Cold War. However, as sovereign nations today, with foreign policy interests, economic priorities, and political goals, these islands can affect and influence great power competition. Looking beyond these nations' relatively small size and economy, the geography of these islands and their proximity to key chokepoints and sea lanes warrants a new perspective in research and writing on the Indian Ocean.

Resources and demography

The Indian Ocean is important not only as a key trading route,[8] but also as a space with coastlines in key sub-regions, ranging from the emerging markets of South Asia and the oil-endowed Middle East to resource-rich Africa. Apart from its trading routes of strategic importance, the Indian Ocean is also home to over 2 billion people with growing economies and growing populations. Instability in any of the sub-regions could potentially alter the geo-economic environment of the immediate area and beyond in terms of trade and engagements, impacting countries in the Indian Ocean rim. The Indian Ocean is also resource-rich and home to some important global fisheries, accounting for "14.55% of the global marine capture harvest."[9] The region supplies nearly "20% of global [tuna] demand worth over USD 6.5 billion annually."[10] As the following chapters of this book will establish, fishing—whether sustainable fishing, illegal and unregulated fishing, or simply fishing vessels—has come to take on a bigger role in the unfolding geopolitics of the maritime domain. Non-traditional security issues, such as illegal fishing, natural disasters, maritime terrorism, drug smuggling, and human trafficking, today have become a part of the repertoire of geopolitical competition, used for purposes spanning from surveillance to influence. This has further pushed the maritime domain into foreign policy engagements and collaborations, underlining the need to study the Indian Ocean as one theater. The use of technologies, such as the Automatic Identification System (AIS)—a navigation system designed to identify and track ships and vessels at sea[11]—and coastal radars, can now address both non-traditional and traditional security issues related to transnational crime and territorial integrity. In twenty-first-century maritime competition, the line between these security issues is quickly blurring, leading to nations vying to gain influence and increase their presence in waters far beyond their territories.

These blurring lines, through the use of similar technology and approaches to address both military threats and maritime crime—such as illegal fishing—further underline the need to study the Indian Ocean as one geographic space. Similarly, as islands increasingly face the challenges of non-traditional security issues, key players looking

to gain influence over them will have to learn to address both traditional and non-traditional security issues. To be able to do that,
countries will have to discard traditional approaches to the study of
competition and conflict. The re-emergence of the Indian Ocean and
the maritime domain within geopolitics also means discarding the
continental geographic division of the Indian Ocean. As Robert
Kaplan describes in his book *The Revenge of Geography*, "at root,
realism is about the recognition of the most blunt, uncomfortable,
and deterministic of truths: those of geography."[12] Geography of the
ocean, its many players, and the islands will reshape the way we
imagine and think of the Indian Ocean. Highlighting the emerging
importance of the Indian Ocean, Kaplan goes on to note, in his book
Monsoon, "If we are entering a phase of history in which several
nations will share dominance of high seas, rather than one as in the
recent past, then the Indian Ocean will play center stage to this more
dynamic and unstable configuration."[13] Kaplan further notes, "The
Cold War forced an artificial dichotomy on area studies in which the
Middle East, the Indian Subcontinent and the Pacific Rim were separate entities."[14] However, in the age of globalization, we must study
the Indian Ocean as one continuous geographic space to identify
new and emerging trends that could potentially alter the way we
think about collaborations and competition in the region. To understand the Indian Ocean dynamics of the twenty-first century, we
must begin by looking at the region as a whole, with a new perspective, one that is better suited for a world 75 years after the end of
World War II.

New players

A new perspective helps identify new players in the Indian Ocean. As
the book looks at the Indian Ocean as one geographic theater, we will
notice the emergence and re-emergence of players such as Saudi
Arabia, the UAE (United Arab Emirates), and Turkey. This helps us

understand the threats and challenges as seen by countries other than the traditional players—primarily the US, India, France, and the UK and, increasingly, Australia and Japan. While China is emerging as the strategic competition for traditional powers in the region, its partnerships with new players as well as the Indian Ocean islands will change the dynamics and the threats for the traditional players and their position in the Indian Ocean. As the book brings in the perspectives and views of the Indian Ocean islands, we will notice the new players, the shifting dynamics, the rise of maritime identities, and the implications of this in shaping a new security architecture in the region. The fact is, the Indian Ocean has many centers of gravity and any nation looking to establish dominant capabilities in the region will have to look at the region as one theater, and the interlinkages between its different nodes. Geography is redefining the Indian Ocean, thrusting it back into great power competition dynamics.

The post-Cold War division of the Indian Ocean led to fragmented policies with nations engaging with its sub-regions in silos. Because of this sub-regional lens, there is a risk of overlooking the emerging trends and factors that have strategic implications. For instance, thinking about Madagascar and Comoros, we tend to think of small developing African nations with little strategic impact. The islands disappear into the larger continental African challenges stripping away their maritime identity. However, once placed in their true geographic setting, as Indian Ocean islands with access to the entire eastern coast of Africa, we begin to see their underlying strategic advantages. A closer look at the islands further reveals Madagascar's increasing political ties with Russia, and Saudi Arabia emerging as a key economic partner for Comoros, as both are Islamic nations. Connecting the dots between Madagascar and Comoros as islands in a key geography with Russia's and Saudi Arabia's evolving partnership with China, we begin to see new trends and developments in the Indian Ocean.

Today, nations with great power ambitions or key Indian Ocean actors looking to maintain their prominence cannot afford to engage with the region in silos. The need to view the Indian Ocean as one continuous geographic space is critical in understanding the geopolitics of the region in the twenty-first century.

The competition with China will be accentuated in the Indian Ocean

The current conversation on conflict is centered on the western Pacific and potential fallout from a Taiwan Strait contingency. It is natural that the US and its friends and allies are preparing for a limited conflict in this theater based on Washington's assessment and view of regional developments. It is true that Beijing has high stakes in the Pacific, particularly in the western Pacific, given its territorial disputes as well as the tense security environment in East Asia. Perhaps this is a bold assertion but this book argues that, while a military conflict might occur in the Pacific, the larger competition will take place in the Indian Ocean. Chapter 3 provides a detailed analysis to reinforce this argument, which examines the Indian Ocean in relation to its chokepoints and economic significance. As a nation with many commitments across the globe, and growing demands on its resources from conflicts in Europe and the Middle East, it is understandable that Washington views strategic developments through the lens of military conflict. However, competition is a long game. The US is preparing for the worst-case scenario, while framing it as "competition," for had it been paying attention, Washington would be quick to realize the Indian Ocean is a sea of vulnerabilities for Beijing, with high economic and diplomatic stakes. Building on the first argument of this book—that the Indian Ocean should be viewed as one continuous theater—this book demonstrates the Indian Ocean is the key theater where the competition (not conflict) with China will be decisive. As well as China's energy dependency—its needs being met via the Indian Ocean—it is also the major route for Beijing's economic, diplomatic, political, and strategic engagements with Africa, the Middle East, South Asia, the island nations, and onward to Europe. Disruptions in the Indian Ocean affect China's ability to forge and expand its global footprint with the wider world. The Indian Ocean is critical to Beijing's wider economic, global, political, and maritime ambitions. China to a great extent has been successful in changing the status quo in the South China Sea, with its artificial islands and more assertive role. It is when Beijing addresses its geographic disadvantages in the Indian Ocean and creates capability to secure its SLOCs and its energy routes that the great power competition will reach a peak. Studying China's interests in the Indian Ocean also involves much more than its "Malacca dilemma," which is a narrow perspective on a worst-case-scenario military conflict. The broader question perhaps is, what does China lose by being absent from the Indian Ocean? This book argues that the Indian Ocean is the theater for Beijing's engagement with Africa, the Middle East, and South Asia, and a key route to Europe, supporting its vision to be a global player. Stronger collaboration with littorals of the Indian Ocean, with whom China has no political baggage, is a necessary component in its competition with the US. The Indian Ocean is also the route to Beijing's deployments to the Atlantic and the Mediterranean, increasing its presence and ability to reach its competitor, the US, through both the Pacific and the Atlantic.

It is my assessment that China's ability to establish a favorable environment in the Indian Ocean will tilt the balance of power toward Beijing in terms of strategic competition. It will be much more difficult to manage competition in the Indian Ocean with a strong China that already has a key position in the western Pacific. Managing this competition in the Indian Ocean will also not be a bilateral engagement, much as in Southeast Asia, where the region will have a voice and role to play. Unlike in the western Pacific, China is a positive player in the Indian Ocean as opposed to western powers with their history of colonial baggage. In this, India, France, Saudi Arabia, the UAE, and Turkey will all play a part in shaping the discourse. To better understand how these players will come to shape the geopolitics of the region, the book goes back to its first argument—the need to study the Indian Ocean as one continuous theater.

Islands' agency will shape great power competition

Viewing the Indian Ocean as one continuous theater helps identify the strategic and geographic significance of the ocean in great power competition, for example, between the US and China. This book makes a third argument, noting that—in studying these evolving dynamics in the Indian Ocean—we must pay special attention to the role of island states in shaping great power competition. This book seeks to explore the role of islands as sovereign nations and its implications for regional and great power competition, in an environment significantly different from that of World War II and the Cold War period. The book argues that island nations are already playing a significant role in shaping great power competition, and will continue to shape the discourse as far as geopolitical competition is concerned.

Chapters 4 and 5 divide the islands of the Indian Ocean into island nations (sovereign states) and island territories (sovereign territories of bigger powers). The island nations are: Sri Lanka, the Maldives, Mauritius, Seychelles, Madagascar, and Comoros. The island territories are: Cocos Keeling (Australia), Andaman and Nicobar (India), Diego Garcia (US/UK/Mauritius), and La Réunion (France). These islands each have their own distinct culture, politics, and identity. Their geography in the Indian Ocean carries varying degrees of implications and influence, together creating a distinct Indian Ocean narrative with a very specific maritime outlook.

One of the key challenges to approaching the Indian Ocean as one theater is the lack of an identity or an Indian Ocean community. Unlike in the Pacific or the Caribbean, the Indian Ocean does not have a shared island community. Similarly, unlike the Pacific with its Pacific Island Forum (PIF), there is also no regional forum advancing the priorities and voicing the challenges of the smaller island nations collectively. The Indian Ocean Rim Association (IORA) is the primary regional structure, including members from Iran to Thailand and Australia to South Africa. The gap in terms of the size of the nations, their economy, and culture means there is more division than unity when it comes to IORA as a regional organization. The Indian Ocean Commission (IOC) brings together Seychelles, Mauritius, Madagascar, Comoros, and La Réunion (France) but not Sri Lanka and the Maldives. As a result, the islands of the Indian Ocean and their voices face consistent difficulties as there is no one platform dedicated to advancing their concerns and challenges. There is also a lack of inter-action among the islands themselves. British and French colonization of the islands meant Sri Lanka and the Maldives adopted English as the official language while Madagascar and Comoros adopted French. Although Mauritius and Seychelles use both languages, French is the primary language for daily conversations. If Sri Lanka and the Maldives associated themselves with South Asia as a region, the other four are African nations with Mauritius and Seychelles balancing the South Asian and African identities.

In the post-1945 world, the Indian Ocean witnessed two domi-nant regional players, with France more active in the western Indian Ocean and the eastern coast of Africa, and India more active in the eastern Indian Ocean and the Arabian sea and the peninsula. Through the Cold War, as countries continued to gain independ-ence, the Indian Ocean emerged as a critical theater for both the US and USSR (Union of Soviet Socialist Republics). Post-Cold War, while the US has remained in the theater, its priorities and interests were focused on developments in the Middle East and its own pres-ence in Afghanistan. The Indian Ocean became an important staging theater for US conflicts, engagements, and priorities in the Middle East and Afghanistan. Over time, this reduced the US to a passive player in the Indian Ocean, despite a significant military presence as the ocean was essentially a key thoroughfare for US interests in the

Middle East and Afghanistan. As the US took on a more passive role in regional developments in the Indian Ocean, France and India strengthened their own roles as key security and economic players in the eastern and western Indian Ocean. For both Paris and Delhi, the other end of the ocean was beyond its respective national interests and capabilities, leading to further division of the Indian Ocean.

The continued division of the ocean further strengthened the lack of interaction among the islands. Although the islands of the Indian Ocean face similar challenges and share common maritime identities, there are limited avenues for them to come together as one community within the Indian Ocean architecture. Michael Pearson, in his book *Indian Ocean*, highlights this lack of identity and the division of the Indian Ocean. Pearson notes, "Most of the population of the littoral states today identify with their state, not with the ocean beyond the borders of the state. If they seek a wider identity, it would not be a maritime one but rather one based on religion, such as Islam, or a wider geography, such as Asia, Africa, the Middle East."[15] Pearson alludes to this division of the Indian Ocean, and the lack of unity or an identity due to the differences and cultures in the sub-regions. The lack of this identity was perhaps especially true between the end of World War II and the beginning of the twenty-first century. However, a closer look confirms the common cultural thread running through the Indian Ocean islands divided primarily by politics and great power interests. This common thread is visible across the island societies of the Indian Ocean influenced by Indian, African, and Arab travelers and merchants, mixed with European colonization in architecture and language. In my travels across these islands, I found the history of the Indian Ocean distinctly present in customs, food, architecture, culture, and language. The islands narrate the story of the people who have traveled through this region influencing food, cultures, and societies. As an Indian Ocean researcher, one of the most interesting intersections of these influences was Comoros: a society where the majority of the people traced their heritage to

15

Bantu communities from eastern Africa, religion influenced by Arab merchants, a cuisine shaped by interactions with Africa, France, the Middle East, and Indian spices, and multiple languages, with French the most widely spoken language. An Indian Ocean island and a member of the Arab league, Comoros has an interesting matrilineal Islamic society.[16]

As these interactions show, throughout Indian Ocean history, all key players of the region have interacted with and influenced the islands, be it the Arabic traders, European colonizers, or India in the post-1945 world. The difference is that today the islands can also influence the key players too.

A maritime identity

As I traveled through the islands conducting research and interviews for the book, I saw more commonalities and similar challenges between all the island states. Yet there was little awareness of shared differences and convergences with islands in the east and west, which were unaware of each other's efforts, cultures, and even societies. This appeared to be due to two factors. First, the islands interacted with the world through their primary partners or at the United Nations (UN). If India and France were prioritizing only one end of the Indian Ocean, so were the island states. While island nations actively participate at the UN, limited resources mean they invest their energy and efforts in dialogue with bigger powers, with capital and resources, to gain their attention, and less time interacting with each other. Second, the islands come together through sub-regional groupings such as the South Asian Association for Regional Cooperation (SAARC) and the African Union (AU) or regional groupings such as IORA. At the multilateral level there are of course groupings such as the Small Island Developing States (SIDS) and Alliance of Small Island States (AOSIS) which bring together islands from different geographies.

To my surprise, my travels through the islands also highlighted the uncoordinated rise of maritime identities, simultaneously among the six island nations of the Indian Ocean. As this book will show, this new identity, one of the Indian Ocean and maritime nation was a result of increasing geopolitical competition, a desire to break away from a single security partner, as well as the re-emergence of the Indian Ocean on the strategic stage. This evolving Indian Ocean identity borrows from each nation's geographic realities, which offer new opportunities as nations compete to gain influence in the Indian Ocean. This is not to say these nations dismissed their island identity in the past; but that a maritime identity was more of a challenge than an opportunity in the post-Cold War era, as sub-regions withdrew to focus on continental troubles. The lack of an Indian Ocean island community meant that Sri Lanka or Comoros found support in SAARC and the AU respectively, rather than in IORA, to voice their concerns and list their priorities. However, the return of the maritime domain as a key geostrategic space brought new opportunities and advantages to the often-neglected Indian Ocean islands.

Although culture, religion, and heritage remain key aspects of Indian Ocean island societies, they are for the first time bound together by a common maritime identity—the Indian Ocean. This shift is a result of a new geopolitical competition, as well as the islands' initiative to play this competition to their advantage. This Indian Ocean identity today provides an opportunity to break out of confined sub-regional groupings dominated by a primary security provider. It paves the way for small island nations to engage with the wider world as Indian Ocean nations rather than within the continental confines of South Asia or Africa. This, in turn, provides solutions ranging from security to economics, allowing expansion of their partnerships from countries beyond the traditional players of the region. These new partnerships with island nations of course carry their own challenges and regional complications, as discussed throughout the book. However, the geography of the islands has become central to the geopolitics of the Indian Ocean.

Conclusion

As I write this book, my ambition is to reconceptualize, rethink, and reframe our mental maps on the Indian Ocean. The following chapters aim to provide a historical background of the Indian Ocean, building on the three main arguments of the book, by placing emphasis on the importance of geography, understanding new players, and the role of islands in shaping great power competition.

Chapter 2 provides a detailed examination of US policy choices toward the Indian Ocean in the post-1945 world amidst its competition with the USSR. As the UK decided to withdraw from east of Suez, Washington began to debate the power vacuum in the Indian Ocean. Chapter 2 draws on US archival documents to underline the geographic importance of the Indian Ocean for great power ambitions through the case of Diego Garcia. This chapter focuses on the rationale for US strategic choices in the Indian Ocean, a distant theater for Washington up until the Cold War. Along with its energy dependency, through developments in its littorals, from the 1967 Arab–Israeli War to the India–Pakistan War of 1971, the United States became more involved, engaged, and concerned about its Indian Ocean policy. This led to Washington writing what is perhaps its only coherent national security memorandum on the Indian Ocean. Diego Garcia remains a unique case in the Indian Ocean, holding more geographic importance in the twenty-first century. This chapter aims to shed light on how great powers think about maritime spaces and highlight the geographic significance of the Indian Ocean for naval powers.

Chapter 3 focuses on the Indian Ocean as one geographic space in the twenty-first century. The chapter attempts to reconceptualize the Indian Ocean, underlining the need to study the ocean as one continuous theater—which powers did during the Cold War, as established earlier in Chapter 2. This chapter sheds light on why China, a rising maritime power of the twenty-first century, will also view the Indian Ocean as one single and continuous theater.

As China views the Indian Ocean as a continuous theater, Chapter 4 demonstrates the role island nations can play in shaping the new great power dynamics across the ocean. This chapter looks at the Indian Ocean from the point of view of island nations: key players of the regional security architecture. It is my endeavor to help readers understand why countries competing for power and influence must rethink and reimagine the Indian Ocean. Moreover, this chapter brings the islands to the center of this debate, to highlight the different aspects of the Indian Ocean that together constitute the changing dynamics of the region. As already stated, the islands of the Indian Ocean today have considerable strategic space to influence great power interactions. That influence is primarily brought about by their geography, making the case for the Indian Ocean to be viewed as one continuous zone in strategic collaborations, and the implications for great power competition.

Chapter 5 makes the distinction between island nations and island territories, and the role each will come to play in defining the security landscape of the Indian Ocean. This chapter focuses on the Andaman and Nicobar Islands (ANI), a group of strategic islands and part of Indian sovereign territory, to demonstrate the role of island territories in naval competition today. If access to Diego Garcia underpinned the priorities of the Cold War period, then the ANI highlight opportunities island territories will come to offer in strategic and military competition in the Indian Ocean. This chapter also captures the shift in power dynamics from the US in the 1970s to India today, in Indian Ocean conversations. This chapter then offers new ideas and arguments in favor of utilizing island territories, creating an island chain across the ocean to establish deterrence and to maintain a balance of power amidst rising tensions between India, China, and the US.

Chapter 6 identifies key issues on the horizon which will come to underpin power dynamics in addressing maritime security challenges. For the Indian Ocean, the Sino-Indian competition, the geopolitics of fishing, and climate change will be instrumental in shaping the regional frameworks, collaborations, competition, and solutions for the Indian Ocean. This chapter also briefly notes developments, such as deep-sea mining, which will drive the next phase of maritime security competition.

It is not my aim to provide a historical account of the Indian Ocean or the islands in the region. This book is not a political study of the islands individually or of their key partners—India, France, or the US. It is about the Indian Ocean as one geographical region, its many players, and the new emerging dynamics. Thus, it takes a focused look at what role islands could play, given their critical geography and their traditional role as key bases for bigger powers aiming to dominate and influence the Indian Ocean rim. Finally, the book is an attempt to generate a new discussion and add to the existing research on the strategic significance of the Indian Ocean and maritime security as a foreign policy tool. On island territories, it argues for utility and that it is worth looking beyond the islands' traditional roles, incorporating issues of the present day to reflect their strategic importance for areas such as Maritime Domain Awareness (MDA), Intelligence, Surveillance and Reconnaissance (ISR), and the implications of non-traditional security issues such as fishing and the blue economy.

The book attempts to make a case for rethinking the nature of geopolitical competition situated within the realms of geography, agency, and multipolarity in the twenty-first century. While history provides innumerable lessons on strategy and statecraft, the competition today is still significantly different. To provide an example of this competition, we only have to look as far as 2022, when the Solomon Islands' decision to sign a security agreement with China initiated a series of policy reactions resulting in the first ever US–Pacific Island summit later that year, and a range of visits and resources for the region, which had gone unnoticed for the previous four decades. This demonstrates the power of agency, where the actions of one small but sovereign nation warranted policy shifts and readjustment of resources to address new developments. In the Indian Ocean, Comoros perhaps holds a similar place, but most policymakers would have struggled to place the island nation on a map until Beijing's agreements did so. This book is an attempt to examine, reassess, and connect the dots in the Indian Ocean to provide a coherent understanding of the developments in the Indian Ocean and their strategic implications for the Indo-Pacific.

2

The Cold War, the Special Relationship, and Diego Garcia

The history of a region or of the interaction of great powers is always helpful in understanding the contemporary dynamics that exist today. The Indian Ocean is no different. As this book attempts to answer the question of why we should look to the Indian Ocean now and, if we do, what are the factors to keep in mind, this chapter aims to contextualize the importance of the region placed in its recent history. This chapter weaves the connections between colonial powers who emerged as key players for newly independent nations, the arrival of the US in the Indian Ocean, a theater from which it was largely absent through the two world wars, and what the region meant for the great power competition—at that time between the USSR and the US. While the USSR no longer exists and the US has prioritized the Pacific as its primary theater, this chapter, through historical records, explains the strategic relevance of the Indian Ocean for countries aiming to be global players and maritime nations. While the players may have changed, with a mix of old, new, and emerging actors, the geographic, strategic, and economic relevance of the Indian Ocean remains and has indeed increased, especially when viewed through the lens of US–China competition, but also through understanding the role nations such as India have been playing, which during the Cold War had limited strategic and military capacities. In doing this, the chapter chronicles the opening of the UK–US military base in Diego Garcia, part of the Chagos Archipelago, at the time Mauritius was moving to independence from the British empire. The military facility marked a significant shift in power dynamics in the Indian Ocean. This chapter attempts to provide an overview of these developments and their implications, to underline the strategic importance of Diego Garcia and the Indian Ocean in the great power competition.

In the post-1945 era, the Indian Ocean emerged as a critical theater for geopolitical competition, especially with the onset of the Cold War between the then superpowers, the United States and the Soviet Union. The superpowers saw each other's presence and deployments into the region as a new and emerging threat, which largely shaped the politics of the Indian Ocean region. While the region was not the primary area or theater for either of the superpowers, it was an ocean that could help them secure their great power status. Beyond direct competition between the USSR and the US, however, the Indian Ocean also underwent significant developments that came to shape the geopolitics of the region and the wider world. From decolonization, which led to new sovereign nations making their sovereign choices, to new naval bases such as the one on Diego Garcia, and the British withdrawal from east of Suez, these developments began to shape the conversations, challenges, and opportunities across the ocean for the coming decades. These very changes laid the foundations for a new geopolitical environment in great power competition in the Indian Ocean. Furthermore, developments concerning new states and the rise of new actors such as India and its engagements with Sri Lanka, the Maldives, Pakistan, and China all had implications for and impact on the affairs of the Indian Ocean. Interactions between newly independent nations and between the superpowers and new players in the Indian Ocean greatly shaped the course of events across the region. In the last decade of the twentieth century, and with the end of the Cold War, the Indian Ocean was also a critical space for US engagements in the Middle East and Afghanistan, situating the region's prominence in extending US air and naval power and in establishing the US as the superpower after the fall of the USSR. Unfortunately, the Indian Ocean has mostly been studied as a critical transit route rather than the theater for competition which affected developments across its littorals.

The "strategic island concept" and British withdrawal

The US Navy in 1959 developed a "strategic island concept," which was approved in 1960, setting the stage for a review and acquisition of new bases and military facilities in areas of importance. The identification and selection of such islands was based on US interests, capabilities, and the presence of hostile nations in the area. Simultaneously, the British government was discussing its defence posture and was leaning toward a withdrawal of its forces from the Indian Ocean and Asia, thereby, creating a "vacuum" in the region, which could be filled by a non-western nation. There were particular concerns in the West about the USSR assuming a greater presence in the region. These two developments laid the foundation for establishing a US presence across the Indian Ocean and the development of the joint US–UK military base in Diego Garcia in the Chagos Archipelago. Diego Garcia is the largest island in the archipelago and had formerly been part of the British Colony of Mauritius.

The 1959 strategic island concept developed by the US Navy is consistent with naval strategies of acquiring offshore bases and facilities on remote islands to defend and protect national interests as well as to project power across large areas of the globe.[1] The island-hopping campaign by the US Navy in the Pacific during World War II was further testament to the utility and need for presence in and access to strategic islands located along sea lines of communications. Throughout the colonial period, when there was a need for such a presence to advance trade and commerce, powers used their navies to colonize critical coastal kingdoms, states, and islands, thereby expanding their empires. Islands located in strategic areas of the maritime domain have always been critical to great power competition and it was no different throughout the 1950s and 1960s as the US and USSR competed for prominence, intensifying the Cold War competition. The withdrawing British military presence only accelerated the need for greater US presence in the Indian Ocean area. However, this theater was relatively new for the US military and policymakers, as Washington traditionally relied on the British government to secure the Indian Ocean, once known as the "British Lake."[2] In January 1966, Robert Komer, US President Lyndon Johnson's deputy special assistant for national security affairs, writing in a memorandum to McGeorge Bundy, the president's special assistant for national security affairs, foresees a growing gap in power projection in the Indian Ocean.[3] Underlining this "weakness" in the Indian Ocean, Komer notes:

> The big remaining issue on the UK defense review seems to be the extent of future British presence in the Suez–Singapore area . . . it seems to me that our larger response must be based on the fact that, viewed globally, the new area where the US itself is militarily weakest is the Indian Ocean area. An even greater vacuum here 1968–75, because of gradual drawdown of the modest UK presence, is worrisome.[4]

The wider argument, then, was about the power vacuum the British withdrawal would create and its consequences for Washington's security concerns. Noting that there has to be some sort of presence in the Indian Ocean, Washington initially proposed asking the UK "to maintain a carrier force in the Indian Ocean":

> whether based in Singapore or Australia. Even one carrier would have real flexibility to meet situations throughout the area (conven-

tional even more than nuclear). If the UK doesn't maintain at least a carrier on station, I predict that the pressures on us to set up an Indian Ocean squadron will increase. No matter how we slice the pie, it would be far more expensive if we had to fill the power vacuum in the Indian Ocean area than to keep the UK there.

Komer's conclusion to the memorandum provides an insight into the developments in the region, and, in particular, the joint project between the US and UK in Diego Garcia. He notes, "my basic point is that looking ahead for the ten years 1966–75 someone (either the US or UK) is likely to have to maintain some flexible sea/air power in the Indian Ocean. It would be far cheaper to subsidize HMG [Her Majesty's Government] than to wake up a few years from now to find that we must substitute for the power vacuum its drawdown of forces creates."[5] This reasoning about a power vacuum and the need to maintain some presence in the Indian Ocean also applies today in the great power competition of the twenty-first century. The players, however, are different in the contemporary context, with China and India playing more prominent roles in the security competition within a much broader US–China contest.

By December 1966, the US and UK had signed a bilateral agreement which provides the US government base rights in the British Indian Ocean Territory (BIOT), which included the Chagos Archipelago, home to the island of Diego Garcia. The US military, during the previous year, in 1965, carried out an assessment of the monetary value of Indian Ocean islands and, in particular, of Diego Garcia and Aldabra, along with Isle des Roches and Farquhar. The US Joint Chiefs of Staff (JCS) in 1965 advised the US secretary of defense: "the military value justifies an expenditure as high as $15 million provided a more favorable alternative financial arrangement cannot be obtained."[6] The US government finally provided $14 million as "detachment costs" for the UK to retain the Chagos Archipelago, Aldabra, Isle de Roches, and Farquhar.

A memorandum dated July 25, 1967, from the US JCS to Secretary of Defense Robert McNamara, titled "proposed naval facility on Diego Garcia," details the importance of Diego Garcia, arguing for the creation of a naval facility on the island. According to the memorandum, which summarizes the JCS examination of the proposal for a naval facility, "Though it would be desirable to obtain UK participation, the US requirement (for a naval facility) for Diego Garcia is such that the project should be undertaken unilaterally, if necessary."[7] At this point, from a defense point of view, the strategic value of Diego Garcia was increasing to a point that there was an argument to construct the facility with or without British collaboration. This memorandum also argues that a naval facility in Diego Garcia would "carry out, partially, the strategic island concept previously recommended by the JCS as a guide for US policy in the Southern Hemisphere."[8] The note provides an insight into the US military perception of the region as well as the importance of the Indian Ocean to US interests. Arguing in favor of a naval facility, the memorandum notes:[9]

> Construction of the facility now is fully warranted. US strategic interests in the area are important and will increase in importance in the future. Political instability of states along the Indian Ocean littoral is likely to continue for many years. Soviet Union infiltration of and pressure on those states are likely to increase, and it can be expected that Communist China as well will increase its efforts to exert influence upon them. An assured base, strategically located in the Indian Ocean, is, therefore, required.
>
> Because of the present lack of assured facilities in the Indian Ocean, the United States is limited in the range of options it can employ in deciding the level of response to a particular threat and, therefore, limited in the effectiveness with which it can protect US interests. The proposed facility would provide the means to support the options for a graduated and flexible response but would not increase US commitments in the area.

Addressing potential questions and concerns on extending US commitments and presence into a new theater by establishing the base, the JCS mention:

> At the same time, a facility on Diego Garcia would be unlikely to embroil the United States in exclusively local problems, because of its isolated geographic location and the political arrangements which the British have made for the islands of the British Indian Ocean Territories.

This line of argument of course appears removed from the course of action taken on the ground to ensure the "isolated geographic location and political arrangements." The population on the island—Chagossians—were forcibly removed, leaving their livelihoods and homes, and barred from coming back. This arrangement of securing the location for a naval facility led to human rights violations, underpinning extended injustices and crimes during the period when nations were gaining independence from colonial rulers.[10]

US archives show there was considerable discussion within the United States government, as well as with the British government, on the nature, process, and importance of setting up a naval facility in the Indian Ocean. Finally, the JCS recommended the following on the issue of constructing a naval facility in Diego Garcia:

> a. Since initial conversations have indicated that the United Kingdom is interested in the facility but is unable to contribute to the cost of construction, an approach be made to the Government of the United Kingdom to ascertain its interest in the following proposals:
>
> (1) The United States to build the facility ($26 million).
> (2) The United States and the United Kingdom to share equally the operating and maintenance costs, estimated at $1.47 million annually.

(3) The United Kingdom to provide the commanding officer, man the facility, and pay manning costs.

(4) The United Kingdom to pay for construction to meet any requirements beyond the US proposal.

(5) Each country to have equal user rights.

b. A decision be made to fund the first increment of construction ($13 million) in the FY 1969 defense military construction budget, regardless of the British decision.[11]

There were also considerable hesitations within the US on the need for an Indian Ocean base. While there was support within the US Navy and wider Department of Defense, there was limited political appetite to establish a new presence in the region. The need for and the importance of a permanent base in the Indian Ocean was repeatedly underscored by the US Navy as well as the JCS. Secretary of Defense Robert McNamara was, however, unconvinced on the need for this base and a US role in the Indian Ocean. On October 26, 1967 he wrote to Secretary of the Navy Paul Ignatius informing the latter of his decision not to approve the "austere" support facility in Diego Garcia as proposed by the navy and recommended by the JCS.[12] McNamara reasons: "Though I accept the principal cost conclusions of the April 15, 1967, Navy study, 'Cost-Effectiveness Analysis of Diego Garcia in Meeting Indian Ocean Contingencies,' I still do not see a clear requirement for the base."[13]

The political conversation on Diego Garcia was also contextualized in relation to the British presence in the Indian Ocean and other remaining bases. The crux of the understanding was that there is only a need for a US base in the region *if* the British withdrew significantly from east of Suez. Underlining this line of reasoning, McNamara noted: "I would be prepared to reconsider the Diego Garcia proposal after we have reached a firm understanding with the British on Aldabra."

In April 1968, the JCS write to McNamara again, underlining new developments in the region and emphasizing the "the necessity for reappraisal of US opportunities, responsibilities, and interests in the Indian Ocean area."[14] The note outlines the JCS decision to re-examine the "political situation and strategic requirements in the Indian Ocean area against the background of events evolving from the Arab/Israeli war and the UK decision to accelerate withdrawal from east of Suez."[15] The note underlines the British role in "stabilizing" the Indian Ocean region, which allowed the US to remain a distant power in the area. They further note the power vacuum created by the "accelerated British withdrawal east of Suez," which will have a direct and long-term impact on the US national interest. There were considerable concerns about the USSR and/or the People's Republic of China (PRC) "capitalizing" on this vacuum. An additional concern, which perhaps was new in great power calculations on national interests, was the actions of newly independent nations. The JCS voice these concerns, noting: "The large number of newly independent nations of Africa and Asia, many with unstable governments and underdeveloped economies, generates political and economic tensions which facilitate Soviet/CPR penetration."[16] These two concerns—greater presence of the USSR and PRC, and newly independent nations—appear to have been the primary concerns and factors shaping US interests in the Indian Ocean from late 1960s onwards. These concerns and questions triggered the process of examining US interests in the Indian Ocean, which led to a series of studies in 1970s—a decade in which the US presence, interest, and engagements in the Indian Ocean as a strategic theater peaked. As the rest of this section demonstrates, this interest was fueled by the USSR presence in the Indian Ocean, and an understanding of what kind of presence the US could create and sustain in the region. The question was, should the US create a naval facility in Diego Garcia (which the political system continued to oppose) and what were the reasons for this, and its interests? Rarely has the US studied the region through a lens other than its competition with the USSR for understanding the strategic importance of the Indian Ocean.

A primary reason for this chapter to draw from archival sources with a focus on Diego Garcia is to underpin the geographic, strategic, and also the military importance of the Indian Ocean. The competition with China—whether on the part of the US or India—has revived questions of the importance of maritime power and the role of the Indian Ocean. Given the limited focus on the Indian Ocean in policy conversations in the recent past, this chapter aims to provide a review of the rationale for and strategic thought on the importance of the Indian Ocean for bigger players embroiled in great power competition. These documents and studies provide an excellent focus for examining the military advantages of the Indian Ocean for a nation aiming to be a maritime power, and why any nation with great power ambitions looks at the Indian Ocean to secure its interests. That conversation is no different today as Washington is engaged in an intense competition with Beijing. Much as in the 1960s, Washington today (both its military and political institutions) struggles to conceptualize the Indian Ocean as one continuous strategic theater, even under its Indo-Pacific strategy, which aims to bring together the Indian and Pacific oceans as one coordinated geostrategic theater. On the other hand, as the following chapters will show, Beijing very well understands the importance of the Indian Ocean and its role in establishing China as a naval power in the twenty-first century—a key pillar of its great power ambitions.

In 1968 the US Navy did understand the value of the region and argued in favor of an Indian Ocean presence. The note from the JCS to McNamara on April 10, 1968 underlines the strategic location of Diego Garcia as well as the need for a presence in the Indian Ocean, arguing:

A joint US military facility on Diego Garcia would provide the United States with a strategically located and politically insulated logistic support and staging base in the Indian Ocean in consonance with the Strategic Island Concept, previously recommended by the Joint Chiefs of Staff, and would serve as a link in an air line of communication in the Southern Hemisphere. The base on Diego Garcia should be an austere military facility capable of supporting limited forces deployed in response to contingency situations and occasional transitors. The central location makes it suitable for support of important functions, such as scientific research, intelligence collection, strategic communications, and strategic ICBM [intercontinental ballistic missile] detection and warning. Appendices A and B hereto contain specific data and rationale.

Emphasizing the strategic location of the Indian Ocean, the JCS underlines:

The Indian Ocean is a critical, strategic area from which large portions of both the USSR and PRC can be targeted from a submarine. Indian Ocean-based ballistic missile systems could expose targets within a 2,100-nautical mile window along the Soviet southern border to an additional threat. This threat would compound Soviet antiballistic missile defenses and further dilute the Soviet antisubmarine warfare effort.

The note concludes by re-emphasizing the earlier JCS note on the need for Diego Garcia as "a valid military requirement," recommending the "approval of immediate establishment of a joint US military facility on Diego Garcia."[17]

Finally, on June 15, 1968, Paul H. Nitze, as the deputy secretary of defense, in a note addressed to the chair of the JCS, the secretary of the navy, and the assistant secretary of defense (ISA), agrees there is a need for a "modest facility at Diego Garcia" after informing the personnel addressed that Nitze saw no justification for the proposal for a $44 million joint major support facility on Diego Garcia.[18] Describing the role and extent of this facility, Nitze writes:

This facility—including ship-to-shore communications, telemetry, scientific, and intelligence monitoring capabilities, and attendant support installations—would provide us increased future flexibility at moderate cost. It could provide a potential backup site in the event that MIDEASTFOR cannot be based at Bahrain after the UK withdraws. In addition, some of our activities at Kagnew Station, Ethiopia, could be transferred to Diego Garcia should the security situation in Ethiopia warrant a reduction in our military presence there.[19] The establishment of the facility would also demonstrate to concerned leaders that we are not totally uninterested in the area.

Should further study reveal that Polaris submarine operations in the Indian Ocean are both feasible and desirable, Diego Garcia could serve as a useful site for replenishment and support. No additional construction or maintenance costs would be incurred in providing such support since the necessary anchorage work would have been accomplished. Moreover, we could in the future move quickly to Indian Ocean basing for Polaris should the Soviet ABM [anti-ballistic missile] capability or ASW [anti-submarine warfare] threat change suddenly.

Consequently, I approve in principle the concept of a modest facility, and the development of a plan for its construction to include austere communications, POL [petroleum, oil, lubricant] storage, an 8000-foot runway and anchorage dredging, at a cost of approximately $26 million.[20]

The US State Department, in a telegram to the US embassy in London, relayed the new agreement for a modest facility on Diego Garcia on condition that "implementation of any agreement [between Washington and London] is subject to final approval and release of funds by USG [US government]."[21] The US embassy in the UK wrote back on September 4, 1968 transmitting their discussion with the British government who were "prepared to agree" to the proposed facility on Diego Garcia, conditioned on the UK flag flying on the facility and adding that British participation will facilitate one or more liaison officers.[22] The British government raised questions on a series of issues which needed to be negotiated before any construction was to begin. Some of the key issues for negotiations were "use of Mauritian and Seychellois labor, and question of resettlement of migrant population." The British government suggested two possibilities: "Removal of population altogether to some locale outside territory, or onto other islands in Chagos group." London also asked for Washington's views on "whether all should move, or whether some of them will be offered employment, during and after construction phase."[23] In the minds of British policymakers, the "difficult question [was] likely to be how and when to make project public knowledge: It will clearly be necessary for both govts [US and UK] to concert closely over this. It is essential to preclude unfavorable reactions by Govts of India and Mauritius by taking them into our confidence before there is any possibility of project becoming publicly known or rumored."[24]

These conversations and agreements led to the current situation on the ground, where the Chagos Archipelago remains uninhabited apart from the presence of military personnel. For decades, the issue of Diego Garcia has remained outside of public view, with little to no knowledge on the details that led to the base being established, as well as the process by which the US gained the location and the facility. This has significant implications in the geopolitical reality of the Indian Ocean today, as many of the nations that were once British colonies have strong views on decolonization as the security environment continues to change. In a particularly difficult position is India, which stands strongly with Mauritius on decolonization while also recognizing the strategic importance and the need for Diego Garcia, amid its own rising tensions with China, which seeks to establish and sustain a presence in the Indian Ocean.

The proposed facility at Diego Garcia and the required funds were to be a part of the US Navy's military construction program for the financial year (FY) 1970. However, it failed to pass Congress as it was "omitted from the FY 70 Military Appropriations Bill by joint Senate–House Committee action during the latter stages of Congressional deliberation on the Bill."[25]

A background paper on Diego Garcia dated February 11, 1970, prepared in the office of the US chief of naval operations states that Diego Garcia was established based on the strategic island concept, which in essence "calls for a stockpiling of islands for contingency use of the US"[26] Providing an overview of the discussions between the US and British governments on BIOT the document notes:

> The BIOT was formed in 1965 and comprises the Chagos Archipelago (includes Diego Garcia), Aldabra, Isle des Roches and Farquhar. The selection of these islands was based on unquestioned UK sovereignty and a negligible native population. The islands were formerly part of the Mauritian and Seychelles groups.
>
> The agreement with the British provides for US use for 50 years with an option for an additional 20 years. The cost of the agreement to the US was one-half of the detachment costs ($14 M) which was funded by offsetting British Polaris R&D charges.[27]

The background note describes how, after the project failed to get approval from Senate, the US Navy made revisions and:

> submitted a modified proposal which is designed to close the gap in reliable communications coverage which exists today in the central Indian Ocean–Bay of Bengal area. Communications services would include the equipment necessary for entry into the Defense Communications System, minimum ship-to-shore radio, a time-shared single channel high frequency rebroadcast facility to serve US shipping and an air–ground flight service. Personnel would be limited to 164 with no facilities for dependents. Support facilities would include an 8,000 ft. runway, minimum waterfront facilities,

personnel support buildings, utilities, POL storage to support the requirements for the facility and dredging to provide a channel and turning basin for deep draft tanker/oiler supply.[28]

Some opposing the project in the Senate were concerned the facility would mean a new visible US commitment in a new area. In response, the background note argues:

The Navy already operates in the Indian Ocean area. The Diego Garcia facility would provide low-profile support to make those operations more economical and efficient. If conditions in the Middle East require us to move out of our Naval Communications Station in Asmara, Diego Garcia is the only foreseeable site in which we can relocate these facilities and preserve our ability to exercise command and control in the Indian Ocean and the Middle East.[29]

Additionally, the navy argued for future operations in the area which could be possible due to Diego Garcia. The navy argued: "The support provided by Diego Garcia would enable us to operate Polaris/Poseidon submarines under the same positive command and control now possessed in the Atlantic and Pacific, and would cause the Soviets to cope with a nearly 360° defense problem. This cannot be construed as increased involvement, but rather, gives us an additional option for our vital sea-based strategic forces."[30] The US Senate finally approved the FY 1971 Military Construction Appropriations Bill on November 25, 1970, which included funding for the "modest BIOT communications facility (Reindeer Station)."[31]

From early 1974, there was a new effort to upgrade the modest facility on Diego Garcia,[32] which also met with resistance from the Senate. The proposed upgrade was considerable from the initial facility. Details of the proposed upgrade are shown in Table 1.

Table 1. US proposal for construction of naval facility on Diego Garcia.

The negotiations for expanded US operational use of Diego Garcia on a long term or permanent basis should include agreement to permit the following:

A.

Facilities principally to support naval operations in the region (cost – $29.05 million).

POL Storage	480,000 Bbls
Power Plant Expansion	2,400 KW
Aircraft Parking Apron	64,750 SY
Aircraft Transit Storage	4,000 SF
Aircraft Arresting Gear	
Ready Issue Ammo Magazine	
Air Transportable Hangar	
Corrosion Control Wash Rack	
Runway Extension	2,000 LF
Cold Iron (MUSE/Fuel/Provisioning) Pier	
Receivar [sic] Bldg Addition	1,250 SF
Air Operating Bldg Addition	2,850 SF
Subsistence Bldg Addition	3,517 SF
BEQ	272 Men
BOQ	32 Men
Cold Storage	4,190 SF
Armed Forces RTS	1,200 SF
General Warehouse	26,385 SF
Crash Fire Station	7,232 SF
Structural Fire Station	3,000 SF
Utilities	

- These improvements constituted the elements of the FY 74 supplemental request to Congress. Labor costs are based on SEABEE construction. There would also be some additional lagoon dredging performed by the contractor now on site.
- Key completion dates for this work, based on an approval to proceed within the next several months, are:
  - Dredging – May 1975
  - Airfield extension and aircraft parking apron – September 1975
  - Power Plant extension September 1975
  - POL storage June 1976
- Completion of these facilities should provide a capability to support:
  - A Carrier Task Group (CTG), an Amphibious Task Group (ATG) with embarked Marine Amphibious Unit (MAU), and associated logistical support ships. Both these groups would be capable of extended operations in the Arabian Sea/Indian Ocean area.
  - A maritime air patrol squadron capable of providing surveillance and/or active operational support of naval units operating in the area.
  - A forward operating location for an Air Force heavy air lift element (C-141/C-5 type) for resupply.

B.

In addition to the naval support effort above, there are under consideration various improvements to the communications network, additional USAF [US Air Force] support capabilities, and some other personnel support items.

A US strategy for the Indian Ocean

On October 3, 1970, US President Richard Nixon and British Prime Minister Edward Heath met in the UK. During their conversation, Heath raised concerns regarding the Indian Ocean, noting, "The Soviets are building up."[33] The British had raised similar concerns earlier, with British Foreign Secretary Sir Alec Douglas-Home expressing his concern "about the possibility of the Indian Ocean becoming a Soviet sea."[34] The conversation between Nixon and Heath in October 1970 became the basis for a series of National Security Study Memorandums (NSSMs) directed by Henry A. Kissinger on the Indian Ocean through much of the 1970s. This decade was a crucial and decisive period in modern Indian Ocean history. The NSSMs led to three specific studies from the US National Security Council (NSC): NSSM 104, titled "Soviet and Friendly Naval Involvement in the Indian Ocean Area, 1971–1975," NSSM 110, titled "Follow-on Study on Strategy Toward the Indian Ocean," and NSSM 199, "Indian Ocean Strategy."[35] A document titled "Indian Ocean Strategy (Response to NSSM 199)" is undated but was likely written between 1975 and 1977.[36] Based on declassified documents to date, and conversations with US NSC personnel between 2008 and 2023, it is likely the Indian Ocean strategy response to NSSM 199 was the last coherent US strategy document on the Indian Ocean.

Simultaneously, Kissinger had begun the series of NSSMs on Indian Ocean with NSSM 104 on November 9, 1970.[37]

"Indian Ocean Strategy" NSSM 199

The primary US economic interests in the region were centered around its access to energy from the Persian Gulf. Its strategic and security interests were attached to the activities undertaken by the USSR in the region. Additional factors were the need to deny advantages to an adversary and to monitor areas of interest. If the USSR was increasing its presence and deployments in the region, then Washington needed to be able to respond. The threat led to the strategy. US interests in the region were also by association with friends and allies, such as Japan and Australia's dependence on the region along with its European allies. The US required stable conditions for its friends and allies so as to be able to secure its own interests across the region. The Indian Ocean strategy (NSSM 199) outlines developments through the early 1970s, such as the India–Pakistan War of 1971, which altered the conclusions of the earlier studies (NSSMs 104 and 110). NSSM 199 describes six developments, urging a review of the conclusions from NSSMs 104 and 110, and the follow-on strategy of NSSM 110. Those developments were: the oil problem; regional conflicts (the India–Pakistan War 1971, Arab–Israeli War 1973); Soviet military activity; the prospective re-opening of the Suez Canal; US forces' presence and support facilities in the Indian Ocean; and arms limitation initiatives.[38]

NSSM 199 notes: "Apart from our new dependence on Middle East oil—an important exception—the conclusions of the earlier studies, that our interests in the Indian Ocean area are moderate but not vital or extensive, are borne out by subsequent events." Later, NSSM 199 identifies five areas that defined US interests in the Indian Ocean in the mid-1970s.

1. SLOCs and access to oil. The studies before NSSM 199 identified the importance of oil imports from the Middle East as to do with the US interest "in the survival of Western Europe and Japan." However, NSSM 199 notes that the use of sea lanes for access to the Persian Gulf must now be added "over an indefinite period for our own [US] economic well being." There was "considerable dis-agreement" among US agencies on the level of the US force posture in the Indian Ocean based on this development. There were two broad arguments, with one group proposing a limited force posture. This group acknowledged and noted the importance of sea lanes from the US to the Persian Gulf as "indisputably vulner-able." However, they did not foresee any capability or interest among the Soviets to interdict international sea lines in order to disrupt US access to the region in a manner that would require considerable military response. The other group argued for an

"Indian Ocean regional military presence adequate to deter Soviet threats to our lines of communication . . ." This analysis was based on (then) existing Soviet military presence and broader Soviet foreign policy objectives which included "control of oil rich nations."[39] This group argued for deterrence by presence.

2. Securing Israel. Although recognizing the distance from Diego Garcia (3,000 nautical miles from Tel Aviv), and the need to secure overflight permissions from Gulf states, the strategy underscored US vulnerability in offering support to Israel "in the face of allied unwillingness to permit us to use their bases for the purpose." The Indian Ocean, in Washington's view, could be "an alternative route for peacetime access and surveillance, and for supply operations if hostilities are renewed, an Indian Ocean staging capability could be seen as a useful adjunct."

3. Balancing the USSR. Capturing the importance of military presence in great power balancing, the strategy notes: "We have a broad interest in not ceding a preponderant military position to the Soviets in the Indian Ocean." The larger question was what would be an appropriate presence and force posture in the Indian Ocean to balance the USSR given the Soviet naval build-up and their presence in the Indian Ocean at that moment.

4. Access to communications, intelligence, and possibly future strategic deployments. This was perhaps a key reasoning for establishing a presence in the Indian Ocean, supporting the argument for Diego Garcia. While the strategy at that point noted the US was yet to deploy SSBNs (ballistic missile submarines), "a breakthrough in Soviet ASW capabilities" would make the region more important for the US.

5. Interests outside of the Gulf. The strategy noted limited interests in the Indian Ocean outside of energy and other resources in the Persian Gulf. It also underlined "unrelenting competition with the USSR for power and influence in the underdeveloped world. We felt this nowhere more keenly than in the Indian Ocean area,

particularly the subcontinent, where US–Soviet competition was treated as a zero-sum game." However, the strategy pointed toward wider acceptance of the Indo-Soviet relationship as long as it does not undermine Washington's broad relationship with the subcontinent. In effect, the strategy did not see a threat from the USSR in its interests outside of the Persian Gulf.

The NSSM 199 strategy examines the region in detail, taking into consideration views, perceptions, and political choices exercised by newly independent nations across its littorals. As a path forward on the question of whether the US needed to increase its presence in the Indian Ocean and, if yes, to what level, the NSSM advised: "Requirements for a significantly increased US force presence in the Indian Ocean depend largely on an interpretation of Soviet strategy in the Middle East. If we judge that the Soviets stand a reasonable chance of using military pressure via the Indian Ocean, together with other means, to secure control of Persian Gulf oil, and thus to gain enormous leverage vis-a-vis the West and Japan, it becomes essential to counter the Soviet challenge." The document then goes on to provide policy alternatives regarding presence through options for (a) low-level, (b) moderate-level, and (c) high-level presence, and by exploring possible arms control through options in tacit restraint, mutual restraint, and formal agreement. Eventually Washington and the USSR entered an arms limitation agreement in the Indian Ocean in the 1980s.

The US Indian Ocean strategy from the 1970s provides a useful insight into considering the Indian Ocean as one theater and reviewing the developments of different corners of the ocean for a complete picture of regional dynamics and strategic threat assessments. This underscores the utility of viewing the Indian Ocean in coordination with the developments in its littorals and sub-regions. The events in the subcontinent, the Persian Gulf and the Arab–Israeli War all had an impact on US interests and assessment of the region, which is no different for a nation with an ambition of maintaining an Indian Ocean presence, such as China. The strongest economic interest was of course energy security, which has changed for the US since it reduced its energy dependency. This view of the Indian Ocean as one theater broke down, especially during the wars in Middle East and Afghanistan, when the US operated without any competition or peer. The Indian Ocean today has changed drastically, and it cannot be viewed through the lens of the decade immediately after the end of the Cold War.

The conversation around US reasoning for increasing its presence in the Indian Ocean included two aspects: first, as a direct response to a perceived growing Soviet presence in the area and second, to follow its own interests independent of the USSR. However, the USSR threat was deemed necessary in order to gain congressional approval for a naval build-up in the Indian Ocean region. Most internal US documents and assessments pointed toward a limited USSR naval presence in the Indian Ocean region, in a manageable context. But the threat was emphasised to win support from Congress. Washington's own reasoning may have come from the British withdrawal and in relation to protection for Southeast Asia. The USSR threat was not necessarily in relation to the sea. It was on land and more aimed toward Southwest Asian nations. An increased US presence at sea was a way to deter the threat emanating from the USSR on land, pointing toward sea-based deterrence for continental threats, which might become a useful lesson today as India and China compete in the Indian Ocean, as well as being engaged in a sovereignty dispute along the continental land border.

With the end of the Cold War, the US war in Afghanistan from 2001 (Operation Enduring Freedom),[40] and the absence of a direct geopolitical competition at the beginning of the turn of the twenty-first century, it is plausible that Washington never reassessed the Indian Ocean through a written strategy, given its diplomatic apprehensions about the strategic relevance of the ocean to begin with.

Today, as the US continues to view China through the lens of competition, the need for a review and a new strategy for the Indian Ocean in the twenty-first century is overdue—especially if the last written strategy dates from the mid-1970s. As this book will demonstrate, an Indian Ocean strategy is not only necessary in order to understand the critical developments of the region in the twenty-first century, but this is also the theater where the competition between today's two great powers will be decisive.

3

Chokepoints and Naval Competition

The Chinese have not yet shown any significant interest in their own use of the Indian Ocean. It is possible they may one day use the region for missile tests, and they could eventually deploy naval ships there.[1]

In the twenty-first century, the Indian Ocean will be the primary theater for competition with China, while the western Pacific will be the main theater in preparation for a conflict. In combination, the Indo-Pacific will be the deciding theater for geopolitical and strategic rivalry in this century. The Indo-Pacific, a strategic concept which encourages the studying of a larger geographic area via the maritime domain, rests on better understanding the Indian and the Pacific oceans and the interactions between the two theaters. The strategic importance of the Indo-Pacific is driven by the movement of goods, commerce, military, and people across the two oceans and between markets, industries, resources, and opportunities. In a more globalized world, the Indo-Pacific concept provides an opportunity to re-study geopolitics and maritime competition through a new lens in the postcolonial and Cold War era. It is an opportunity to redefine our mental maps of sub-regions reinforced by the developments of the post-Cold War era and to understand the implications of developments in one ocean on the other and, by extension, at a global level. The Indo-Pacific concept helps us understand why competition with China, a Pacific power, will play out in the Indian Ocean. As former prime minister of Japan Shinzo Abe, also an architect of the Indo-Pacific concept, notes, it's about the confluence of the two seas[2] and its influence on global politics.

The wider Pacific Ocean attracts greater attention and more narratives within the Indo-Pacific strategic construct, although the latter gives the opportunity to study two oceans and the interactions therein. The reason for this is that the competition is largely between the US and China, and both nations border the Pacific Ocean. There is, however, a unique case to be made regarding the strategic importance of the Indian Ocean and its implications for Pacific powers and actors. Although the western Pacific is the home theater for China, a new growing maritime power, it has greater stakes, interests, and, most importantly, vulnerabilities in the Indian Ocean in terms of its global economic, military, and diplomatic engagements. Without securing its interests, investments, and stakes in the Indian Ocean, Beijing will remain in a disadvantageous position in its competition with the US. Without securing its position and sea lanes of communication in the Indian Ocean, China will fall short in realizing its vision of becoming a maritime power. For the Indian Ocean is China's sea of vulnerabilities in relation to its stakes and interests in establishing itself as a key security and political player in the Indo-Pacific and beyond.

The maritime domain has regained its significance in the twenty-first century in great power geopolitics. The Gulf War, the war in Afghanistan, instability in the Middle East, and continental challenges in Africa and South Asia, all pushed the Indian Ocean and the maritime framing of the region to the periphery of geopolitical conversations and decisions in the latter half of the twentieth century. Disputes along continental borders, and the relative calm in the maritime domain, contributed to the lack of consideration of the importance of maritime security and the role of the maritime domain in geopolitical conversations. Outside of all the navies of the world, very limited importance has been placed on studying the significance of the maritime domain in understanding new challenges and trends, particularly for the twenty-first century. The lack of a crisis, and the absence of direct competition in the Indian Ocean after the disintegration of the USSR, led to further continentalization of world issues. This led to the adoption of a continental view of maritime issues, creating silos across vast spaces of the ocean.

The Indian Ocean is the primary ocean of vulnerabilities for Beijing in comparison to its stakes and interests across the Indo-Pacific. Not only does China depend on the Indian Ocean for nearly 80% of its energy requirement,[3] but it is also the main ocean for China's political, military, and economic engagements with Africa, the Middle East, South Asia, and the island states. If China wants to be a credible player in Africa, it needs a stable and secure Indian Ocean. If China wants deeper economic ties with the Gulf nations, it needs a stable and secure Indian Ocean. If China wants to be considered a serious player for the island nations, it needs a stable and secure Indian Ocean. However, to be considered a key player for these sub-regions, Beijing also needs to be able to operate and sustain itself across the Indian Ocean, fly its flag consistently, and be engaged in addressing regional challenges from search and rescue to anti-piracy missions. The desire and need to maintain, sustain, and operate in the Indian Ocean uninterrupted turns the theater from a region of interests to one of competition for Beijing. As Beijing scales up its presence, efforts, and engagements across the Indian Ocean both Sino-Indian competition and US–China competition will intensify. Given that both Delhi and Washington have better presence and capabilities in the Indian Ocean, it will become necessary for Beijing to build capabilities, with the goal of protecting its own SLOCs, chokepoints, and, most importantly, its economic and strategic engagements across the wider ocean. While China is unlikely to enter into a military conflict with anyone in the Indian Ocean, particularly within the next five-to-ten-year time frame, a more effective deterrence for Beijing in the western Pacific in that same time line might lie in the Indian Ocean—China's area of weakness, but also of great significance. A review of Indian Ocean geography through its chokepoints and SLOCs will help in understand its importance.

Sea power and sea lines of communication

Perhaps for most naval theoreticians, command of the sea meant control over sea lines of communication.[4]

Naval dominance is intricately related to the security of chokepoints in the maritime domain. Depending on the nation's trading pattern and economic engagements, the ability to protect its SLOCs is fundamental to the nation's economic growth while protecting its strategic interests. Often, a navy's primary goal is to protect its SLOCs across vast oceans and seas to safeguard its nation's economic interests. A nation able to protect its own SLOCs across multiple oceans and to provide security to its friends and allies could emerge as a dominant maritime power. A nation's ability to protect its own SLOCs as well as to disrupt its adversaries' SLOCs running across its key trading routes is important in a country's quest to become a superpower. While there are many elements that contribute toward a nation's ambition to be a maritime power, its ability to protect its trade routes is a primary necessity. In the maritime domain, SLOC and chokepoint protection are necessary missions for the navies of the world, during times of both peace and conflict.

Sea control and sea denial are complex terminologies and naval theorists have contributed much to the literature in exploring the different aspects of these concepts and their relevance to and importance in naval campaigns and wars.[5] It is connected to the importance of a chokepoint in winning naval campaigns, however. As Milan

Vego notes, "The concept of sea control is at the same time both simple and complicated. In its simplest definition, sea control can be described as one's ability to use a given part of the ocean/sea and associated air (space) for military and nonmilitary purposes and to deny the same to the enemy in a time of open hostilities."[6] The purpose of sea control, Vego notes, is to facilitate "the defense and protection of friendly maritime traffic and denies the same to the enemy. Economic exploitation of sea control can contribute greatly to ultimate victory in a war."[7] On the importance of chokepoints, Vego underlines, "Straits, or 'choke points,' have had a very great importance in the struggle for sea control throughout the ages. Choke point control is only the first although the most important step, for obtaining control of a given enclosed or semi-enclosed sea theater."[8] Sea control, sea denial, SLOCs, and chokepoint control are all inter-related and the degree of relevance for each differs based on the mission and purpose. In the twenty-first century, as we seek to better understand the implications of great power competition, the rise of China, and its rivalry with the US and India, these concepts and notions come back into play, albeit within the context of advanced naval technology and a world order that differs significantly from that of the colonial and Cold War eras. Viewing the Indian Ocean through its geography of chokepoints will help us understand the role and implications of this ocean in global developments.

During World War II, Japan's capture of Singapore enabled its ability to secure the Strait of Malacca, the passage connecting the Indian Ocean to the Pacific. That, in turn, supported Japan's capture of Indonesia, Burma, and the Andaman and Nicobar Islands, further strengthening the Japanese foothold along a critical chokepoint. Later, Imperial Japan bombed Sri Lanka (then called Ceylon), a key base for the British empire, resulting in the British fleet leaving the island and retreating to the western Indian Ocean.[9] Imperial Japan's control of a chokepoint played a critical role in pushing the British to the western coast of the Indian Ocean, from an area the British

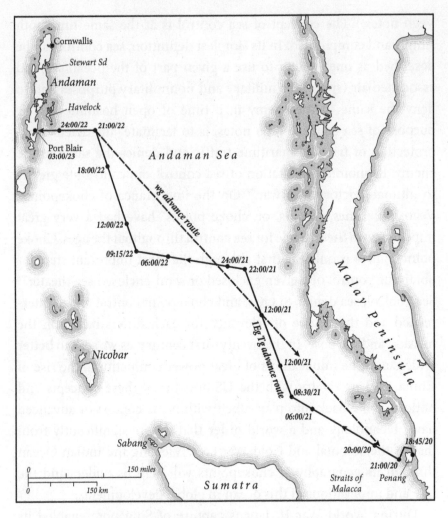

Map 2. Imperial Japan's capture of the Andaman and Nicobar Islands.

empire had dominated almost unchallenged for over 150 years. Ultimately, the ability of the US to capture and disrupt Japan's SLOCs across the Pacific was instrumental in winning the war against the Imperial Japanese Navy. In the Cold War era too, as the previous chapter underlines, the presence of the Soviet Navy greatly impacted US policies in the region and vice versa. Washington's interests in the Indian Ocean included its ability to protect shipping and energy lines for its friends and partners and to deter the Soviet Navy through presence. SLOC protection and chokepoint control have been, and will remain, crucial factors for any nation's ambition to be a maritime power. The strategic significance of the Indian Ocean, throughout its history, has been about geography, chokepoints, and SLOCs. In the twenty-first century too, competing powers such as the US and China will find themselves jostling for power in this ocean, although they are both Pacific nations. The chokepoints and SLOCs across the Indian Ocean will come to play an important role in both building capabilities and creating deterrence. Chapter 5 discusses in detail the role of island territories for Indian Ocean security.

Most naval battles and campaigns throughout World War II and before that have been linked to a nation's ability to protect its own and disrupt its adversaries' chokepoints and key SLOCs. Studying great power competition at sea through chokepoints provides a unique perspective. The Indian Ocean, when viewed through its chokepoints of Bab-el-Mandeb, the Strait of Hormuz, and the Strait of Malacca, tells a compelling story of its strategic importance for the twenty-first century. Moreover, to understand a maritime domain and its implications for geopolitics, it is worth studying the ocean as one continuous space, with the littorals and islands as its actors, rather than viewing the ocean through the prism of continental silos.

Chokepoints and blind spots

> Do you know that there are five keys to the world? The Strait of Dover, the Straits of Gibraltar, the Suez Canal, the Straits of Malacca, the Cape of Good Hope. And every one of these keys we hold.[10]

One of the pressing challenges of the Indian Ocean has been a continental framing of a maritime space in relation to South Asia, the Middle East, and Africa. To better understand the geography and strategic significance of the ocean, it is useful to examine the region

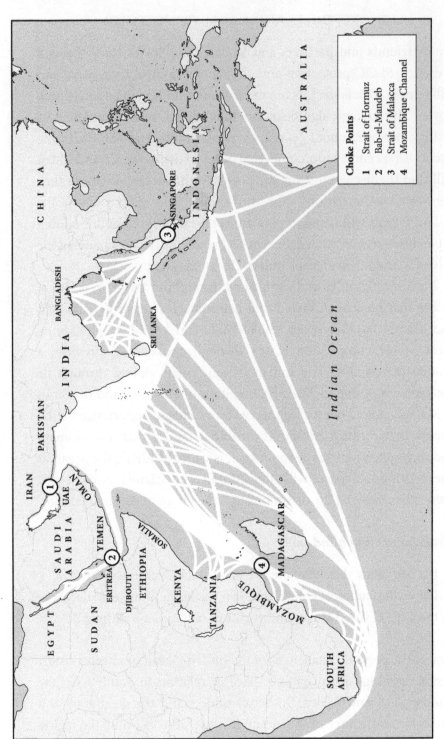

Map 3. Chokepoints and energy transit in the Indian Ocean.

through chokepoints and connecting waterways. A chokepoint, in its simplest definition, is a bottleneck, a narrow passage connecting two wider spaces. A maritime chokepoint or a strategic chokepoint refers to a narrow passage between two seas or oceans with limited alternative routes and sometimes, without any practical alternatives. The military significance of a chokepoint increases when the passage is a dominant trade route between two key destinations and where the alternative is either impractical or incurs significantly higher economic costs. Vego notes, "The principal objectives in establishing choke point control are to prevent the enemy surface combatants/submarines and military/commercial shipping from operating outside the confines of a given enclosed or semi-enclosed sea, to destroy the enemy fleet within a strait, and to capture one or both shores of a strait/narrows."[11]

The US Energy Information Administration (EIA) identifies seven major trade routes as critical for global seaborne oil transportation.[12] These routes include straits and chokepoints that together account for majority of oil and energy movement across the world. The seven trade routes and chokepoints are:

- Strait of Hormuz
- Strait of Malacca
- Suez Canal and Sumed pipeline
- Bab-el-Mandeb
- Danish Straits
- Turkish Straits
- Panama Canal
- Cape of Good Hope

As per the EIA, the seven chokepoints are identified based on their importance in facilitating seaborne transportation of oil.[13] Underlining the economic value of these chokepoints, the EIA notes, "Disruptions to these routes could affect oil prices and add thousands of miles of transit in alternative routes." Among the seven identified above, "By volume of oil transit, the Strait of Hormuz, leading out of the Persian Gulf, and the Strait of Malacca (linking the Indian and Pacific oceans) are the world's most important strategic choke-points."[14] Both are in the Indian Ocean. Out of the seven, the Indian Ocean is home to three critical energy chokepoints—Hormuz, Malacca, Bab-el-Mandeb—and two secondary trade routes and chokepoints which directly connect the Indian Ocean to a region beyond the ocean—the Suez Canal and the Cape of Good Hope. In essence, out of the seven most important energy chokepoints in the world, five can be accessed from the Indian Ocean and are directly connected to waters in the region. If sea control and sea denial are executed around strategically important chokepoints and SLOCs, then the geographic importance of the Indian Ocean is evident given its importance for movement of global trade. The ability to disrupt any of the five chokepoints in the Indian Ocean will have significant consequences not just for the region but globally. Similarly, any nation that perceives a threat toward its critical SLOCs through the Indian Ocean will find it compelling to build capabilities to defend and protect those sea lanes.

A closer examination of these chokepoints' geography and signif-icance can help underscore the need to understand and study the Indian Ocean region as one continuous maritime theater and why the ocean will become central for competition with China. For the scope of this book, the critical chokepoints are the Strait of Hormuz, Bab-el-Mandeb, and the Strait of Malacca. To highlight the impor-tance of geography and connectivity, the author believes it is also important to look at the Red Sea/Suez Canal and Indonesian straits, as well as the Mozambique Channel, while discussing geopolitics of the Indian Ocean.

The EIA considers the Strait of Hormuz and the Strait of Malacca as the "world's most strategic chokepoints."[15] The Strait of Hormuz alone accounts for "21 million barrels per day (b/d), [in transit] or the equivalent of about 21% of global petroleum liquids consumption."[16] As per a 2017 report, the four chokepoints mentioned above see the movement of 47 million barrels per day of crude oil and petroleum products, out of a total of 97.2 million barrels per day that transit the nine key chokepoints to markets across the globe.[17] Any disruptions, let alone a blockade of these chokepoints, would have catastrophic consequences for the world economy and nations dependent on energy transiting through these sea lanes.

Strait of Hormuz

The Strait of Hormuz connects the Persian Gulf to the Indian Ocean. It is bordered by Iran to the north and the UAE and Saudi Arabia to the south. Iraq, Iran, Kuwait, Saudi Arabia, Qatar, Bahrain, and the UAE all have a coast along the Gulf, with the Strait of Hormuz being the only waterway connecting these littorals to the Arabian Sea, the Indian Ocean, and beyond. Oman sits at the eastern mouth of the strait. In terms of its significance for energy transits, the EIA by its own estimates underlines the strategic importance of the chokepoint for global trade and in particular for "petroleum liquids consumption"[18] In terms of markets, the EIA notes, "about 80% of the crude oil that moved through this chokepoint went to Asian markets, based on data from Lloyd's List Intelligence tanker tracking service. China, Japan, India, South Korea, and Singapore are the largest destinations for oil moving through the Strait of Hormuz."[19] The Persian Gulf and the Strait of Hormuz have inadvertently become an important area of interest not only for access to energy suppliers but also because of the implications for the Indian Ocean. Given that the Middle East accounts for 50% of China's crude oil supply, Beijing's desire to be able to secure its SLOCs and energy routes to and from this region is only natural and will grow with time. Given the maritime nature of this route and access, it is important to consider developments in this region within the geographic realities of Indian Ocean chokepoints, rather than as only a Middle East development, which immediately draws continental maps in the minds of most policymakers. The Middle East has a significant maritime component within the Indian Ocean theater. Major economies and markets in Asia and Europe depend on continued access to these waters for their energy demands.

Bab-el-Mandeb

Bab-el-Mandeb is a narrow passage or a chokepoint that connects the Horn of Africa in the Indian Ocean to the Mediterranean Sea via the Red Sea. It is bordered by Yemen to its north and Djibouti to its south. This is the primary route for trade and movement of goods between Europe, the Middle East, and Asia. To contextualize the significance of this chokepoint, the Suez Canal will be significantly less important if the Bab-el-Mandeb is disrupted. The alternative to this route is via the Cape of Good Hope and through the Mozambique Channel—a key route prior to the opening of the Suez Canal.[20] This chokepoint facilitates movement of trade and, in particular, oil between Europe and Africa to Asian markets. The Suez Canal was disrupted in March 2021, when a container vessel ran aground in the narrow passageway, halting traffic for about a week.[21] As per estimates, the incident cost $9.6 billion per day in commercial seaborne traffic.[22] Routing around the Cape of Good Hope as an alternative to the Bab-el-Mandeb and the Suez Canal adds approximately three weeks to a shipping journey, increasing costs, including insurance.

Strait of Malacca

The Strait of Malacca is perhaps one of the most important and well-known maritime chokepoints of the twenty-first century. The strait is bordered by Singapore, Malaysia, and Indonesia, and is the key passage for connecting the Indian Ocean to the South China Sea and the Pacific. It is the main artery connecting Europe, the Middle East, and Africa to China, Japan, and South Korea, as well as all Southeast Asia. The Strait of Malacca is geographically, economically, and strategically important to keep sea lines of communications open, secure, and stable, not just for China's interactions with countries across the Indo-Pacific but also for Europe, Africa, the Middle East, and South Asia's interactions and movements of goods with Southeast, East, and Northeast Asia.

Mozambique Channel

Although not a traditional chokepoint, the Mozambique Channel is an important route and a key alternative, should the Suez Canal be inaccessible. Prior to the opening of the Suez Canal, the Mozambique Channel was the key route for movements between Europe, the eastern coast of Africa, the Middle East, Asia, and Australia, rounding the Cape of Good Hope. Its strategic relevance is likely to re-emerge as we see growing competition over influence and access to African nations as well as potential hydrocarbon resources in the channel. Bordered by Mozambique and Madagascar, with Kenya and Comoros sitting on its northern mouth, this sub-region is likely to see increased attention in the coming decades. France is a key player in the area, with Exclusive Economic Zones (EEZs) generated by the scattered islands, some of which are in dispute with Madagascar.[23]

Beyond the Malacca dilemma

China's Malacca dilemma is comparatively well known.[24] The dilemma underlies Beijing's difficult choices in SLOC protection between the Indian and the Pacific Ocean, a route critical for China's energy security and ties with the littorals of the Indian Ocean region. The dilemma is that Beijing has growing trade and economic stakes in the Indian Ocean but limited presence in the theater to secure its SLOCs. A safe, secure, and open Strait of Malacca, one of the most critical energy chokepoints in the world, is central to Beijing's economic growth and energy security. Beijing has long been wary about the possibility of China's adversaries—whether it be India or the US or their partners and friends—disrupting China's access to the Indian Ocean by limiting the flow and movement of goods through the Strait of Malacca. Can China continue to depend on a secure Indian Ocean to protect its SLOCs without building its own capabilities and military presence in the Indian Ocean? If China moves forward in building its military presence and deployments in the Indian Ocean, can it do so without creating concerns in Washington and Delhi? Most importantly, if Beijing does not build its capability to secure its own SLOCs in the Indian Ocean, can it access its energy lines during a time of conflict, whether it be with Delhi, Washington, or another power? What is the implication of SLOC security across the Indian Ocean during a Taiwan Strait contingency? The dilemma writes itself.

While China's Malacca dilemma is widely understood, the Strait of Hormuz and the Bab-el-Mandeb are equally crucial for energy transits in the Indian Ocean. Without a secure Hormuz and Bab-el-Mandeb, there will be no energy to be transported through the Strait of Malacca for nations in Southeast and East Asia, including China.

So how dependent is Beijing on the Indian Ocean for its access to energy lines? According to the US Energy Information Administration in 2022, the Middle East accounts for 50% of China's crude oil imports.[25] In the Middle East, Saudi Arabia accounts for 17% of China's crude oil imports, Iraq 11%, Oman 9%, Kuwait 6%, the UAE 6%, and Qatar 2%. After the Middle East, as per 2021 data,[26] Russia is the second largest crude supplier, accounting for 15% of China's crude oil imports. China also imports from Angola (8%), Colombia (2%), Brazil (6%), Congo (2%), Europe (4%), and the US (2%). Geographically, China imports 50% of its crude oil from the Middle East, 13% from the African continent, 15% from Russia, and 15% from the Americas, the majority of it from South America.[27] The

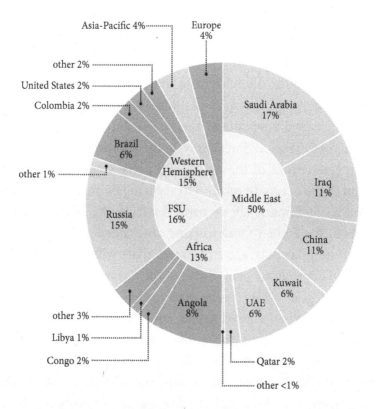

Figure 1. China's crude oil imports by source, 2021.

Note: Total may not equal 100% because of independent rounding. FSU (Former Soviet Union) refers to countries that once made up the Soviet Union.

Source:, EIA from Global Trade Tracker data

Indian Ocean is the primary theater for China's access to its top crude oil suppliers and secondary for others. Over 70% of China's crude oil transits the Indian Ocean and its chokepoints. Beijing's dilemma well transcends the Strait of Malacca, particularly during peacetime. The Strait of Hormuz and the Bab-el-Mandeb connecting the Red Sea to the Suez Canal are equally important for China's growth as well as its expanding economic, political, military, and diplomatic footprint.

When viewed through the geography of the maritime domain and its chokepoints, the Indian Ocean is China's sea of vulnerabilities (see

Map 3). The competition, therefore, will accentuate in the Indian Ocean region as China seeks to build its global maritime profile while the US and its partners jostle to retain their place as traditional and legacy players within the changing dynamics of the region in the twenty-first century. The next chapter discusses the role of island nations and island agency and their contribution to the changing geopolitics of the region. Put simply, in the coming decades, developments in one corner of the ocean will carry consequences for the other end of the ocean. In relation to securing Beijing's energy transition, and its diplomatic efforts toward Africa, the Middle East, and South Asia, the Indian Ocean is one and connected. The ocean is critical for Beijing's outreach and connectivity with Europe as well. A divided and continental perspective of the ocean offers only a partial view of the region, while it also undermines the importance of the Indian Ocean. When viewed as one continuous geographic theater, the Indian Ocean, its major chokepoints, and the Mozambique Channel together comprise the sub-regions of the Persian Gulf, the Middle East, the Horn of Africa, and the eastern coast of Africa, South Asia, and the island nations; all are accessed primarily through the Indian Ocean. The ability to maintain and sustain a naval presence across these sub-regions would carry significant geopolitical, diplomatic, and military weight for a nation aiming to be a global maritime power. Combined with the islands of the Indian Ocean— Sri Lanka, the Maldives, Mauritius, Seychelles, Madagascar, and Comoros—the Indian Ocean is home to some of the most strategically located nations along key trading routes bordering the most critical chokepoints for oil and energy transits in the world.

Connecting the silos

A critical challenge in assessing developments in the Indian Ocean is the continental division of a maritime domain. The ocean is often divided into the continental sub-regions of Africa, South Asia, and the Middle East, which poses a challenge to thinking of the strategic importance of the ocean as one theater. For example, each of these sub-regions has considerably different geopolitical developments and actors, with many different challenges emerging in continental Africa, the Middle East, and South Asia. When discussing South Asia or Africa, the immediate attention goes toward developments on land resulting from continental border crises or conflicts. Given that each continent has very different dynamics, they are also studied in silos so as to provide each one with the attention its issues deserve. However, in the process, the maritime developments attract far less geopolitical attention. While there might not be overlaps or a connection between border disputes and conflicts in South Asia and Africa, there are correlations between developments in Sri Lanka and Mauritius, whether they concern economic and development partnerships or shared challenges regarding climate change or illegal fishing. Therefore, a study of the Indian Ocean through its continental sub-regions has greatly impacted the strategic developments across the maritime domain in the twenty-first century. While India, the US, Australia, and others are commonly understood to be important players in the Indian Ocean today, we rarely study the impact or rise of Turkey, the UAE, or Saudi Arabia as Indian Ocean players, all emerging and important players for the region today.[28]

Take for example the US Department of Defense (DoD), which approaches the Indian Ocean through three combatant commands: INDOPACOM, CENTCOM, and AFRICOM. Out of the three commands, only one, INDOPACOM, has a dominant naval outlook or a maritime approach. In essence, INDOPACOM would be the nodal point for Indian Ocean coordination for the US military. However, bureaucratically, the command's Area of Responsibility (AOR) ends with India, leaving out the entire central, southern, and western Indian Ocean from its purview. There are good reasons for such a division in Washington's approach, spanning across questions of priority (mostly in Pacific and East Asia), resources, and the importance of the Indian Ocean. While there are many arguments to be made in favor of the strategic importance of the Indian Ocean, one that perhaps underlines its prominence in the twenty-first century is as a key theater for naval and, in turn, geopolitical competition. As far as competition with China goes, Beijing's dependency on the region spans energy, economic, military, and political interests. Besides the fact nine out of the top ten countries[29] that supply China's crude oil are reliant on the Indian Ocean for movement, the ocean is also critical for Beijing's engagements (political, diplomatic, economic) and access to Africa, the Middle East, South Asia, and the islands of the Indian Ocean. It is one theater where Beijing has an equal number of stakes and vulnerabilities. Securing the Indian Ocean and sustaining the Chinese presence across the ocean is critical to Beijing's maritime as well as global ambitions. It is the ocean where China's first overseas military facility was built. However, due to the artificial continental division of the ocean, developments such as the Chinese naval facility in Djibouti are understood more as an Africa development than an Indian Ocean development, undermining the importance of the region. While it is often assumed that Pakistan, Sri Lanka, Myanmar, or Cambodia will host the next Chinese base, it is perhaps the western Indian Ocean that provides better strategic rationale for a Chinese facility.

While the US and its partners continue to look at the Indian Ocean as divided into continental silos, Beijing, for its part, has been consistent in its presence across the region. For example, China is the only nation with an embassy or a diplomatic mission in each of the islands in the Indian Ocean. Recent reports about a potential Chinese facility in the UAE, Wang Yi's visit to Comoros, and the recent China–Indian Ocean Region Forum, all underline Beijing's interest in the ocean as well as the maritime blind spots across the Indian Ocean. While developments in Sri Lanka, Pakistan, or Myanmar gain considerable attention, developments in the western Indian Ocean go relatively unnoticed. From a strategic viewpoint, a second Chinese military facility in the western Indian Ocean, and potentially in Comoros or Madagascar, could be both feasible and sustainable. These islands and the strategic chokepoints tend to go unmentioned and unnoticed in understandings of Beijing's maritime outreach and dependencies, and their relevance to the strategic importance of the Indian Ocean is overlooked. Growing partnerships between China and nations such as Saudi Arabia, Turkey, and the UAE will also provide new opportunities for Beijing's engagements in the region. It might also be worth noting that Russia's plan to set up a military facility in Sudan on the Red Sea coast, before its invasion of Ukraine, signals a new maritime competition in the Indian Ocean. To truly understand the importance of the Indian Ocean and its implications for great power competition today, we must study the region as one continuous maritime domain instead of through the continental silos that emerged through the Cold War.

Geography plays an underlying and unalterable role in geopolitical competition. The continental division of a maritime domain[30] created silos within the Indian Ocean, separating the challenges and implications that emerged in one corner of the ocean from those that emerged in another. As we connect the silos, and view the ocean through the prism of chokepoints and sub-regions, a larger picture comes into focus. The Indian Ocean is China's theater of vulnerabilities. Given the flow of goods and traffic, combined with its energy dependency on the Persian Gulf, Beijing will increasingly feel the need to be present and secure the Indian Ocean. It is the ocean in which China is relatively weaker militarily than in the western Pacific and the South China Sea. Until Beijing builds its capabilities to secure its SLOCs in the Indian Ocean—or finds an alternative route to the Persian Gulf, Africa, and South America—the Indian Ocean will remain China's sea of vulnerabilities. Building in an assumption that, in the future, China might have reduced energy dependency on the Persian Gulf, as a key actor and player, the Indian Ocean remains strategically important for engagement with Africa, Europe, the Middle East, and the island nations.

In the twenty-first century, competition with China will come to the fore in the Indian Ocean, for it is in the Indian Ocean that China has higher stakes and the need to establish itself as a key actor beyond its immediate region. Beijing's presence in the Pacific is critical for its defense and in creating deterrence for its competitors, be it Japan or the US. However, China's presence in the Indian Ocean is necessary for its own growth, including its economic and energy security as well as to increase its global footprint. China is unlikely to become a great power without creating and sustaining a presence in the Indian Ocean. Its stakes and vulnerabilities are of crucial significance to China's economic and military growth and expansion. As noted by Chinese scholars, "The maritime arteries connecting China's economy with the outside world are almost constantly under deterrence and intimidation by other maritime powers."[31] Connecting the silos perhaps points us toward the most effective theater to create deterrence for China— the Indian Ocean. A limited or military conflict could potentially take place in the western Pacific or the Indian Ocean decades from now if China is able truly to create a strong, effective, and sustainable military presence as the US was able to during the Cold War, but the competition, leading up to a full conflict, will take place in the Indian Ocean.

On sustaining a military presence in the Indian Ocean, two or more facilities in the Indian Ocean could secure China's presence there, even with a looming threat over the Strait of Malacca. A second base in the Indian Ocean would make sustaining a presence across the ocean more feasible and effective. Djibouti was constructed with a focus on anti-piracy missions; the next military facility will perhaps clarify how China views its interests and investments in the Indian Ocean. A second Indian Ocean base from Beijing is simply a matter of time. Although there is more concern expressed about a potential Chinese military facility emerging in the eastern Indian Ocean, a second facility on the western Indian Ocean will also carry important geostrategic consequences. A second facility will enable sustained and more committed engagements across the wider Indian Ocean. Due to the disconnect in understanding the Indian Ocean, a facility in the western Indian Ocean will be understood to be another Africa development, similar to the one in Djibouti. A facility in the southwest Indian Ocean, somewhere between Djibouti and Mozambique, would provide space for Beijing to step up its engagement without drawing too much attention from other traditional players, except France. As a key player in the western Indian Ocean, Paris closely monitors developments there. An indication of China's presence and keen eye on the region is perhaps then Foreign Minister Wang Yi's visit to Comoros in early 2022. The island nation, strategically situated in the northern Mozambique Channel, between Madagascar and Kenya, could become a flashpoint just like the developments in the Pacific in 2022 did, regarding the Solomon Islands' security agreement with China.[32] Comoros is located close to Mayotte, a French overseas territory which Moroni (capital of Comoros) claims as its sovereign territory. A facility in Djibouti, supported by another potentially in Comoros, would also provide a certain degree of airpower in the southwest Indian Ocean covering the Bab-el-Mandeb, the Strait of Hormuz, and the Mozambique Channel. The region is so poorly understood in terms of maritime security and great power competition that developments in these areas could also potentially go unnoticed.

It is worth noting that a Chinese presence in the Indian Ocean is unlikely to be combat-ready for a two-ocean conflict in the near future, if ever. Increased advantages in the Indian Ocean, however, will embolden China in the west and south Pacific if geopolitical competition continues to increase. In the Indian Ocean, Beijing will compete with traditional and legacy players like France, India, or the US. China's advances in the Indian Ocean could serve as preparation to address its obvious vulnerabilities there and to present itself as an alternative, or addition, to efforts driven by France, India, and the US. If China wants to present itself as a credible security player in the Indian Ocean, Beijing will feel the need to be able to fly the flag consistently. A sustained presence in the Indian Ocean, which could reinforce both its anti-piracy efforts and its continuous engagements with littorals and islands in the region, will help Beijing deepen its engagement in and understanding of the region while also improving its own experience of operating there. A second Chinese military facility in the Indian Ocean is very likely and would be a logical development of Beijing's increased engagements and investments across the ocean. Such a facility, particularly in the western Indian Ocean, will strengthen Beijing's presence and engagements closer to the Red Sea and eastern coast of Africa. It would also complement the existing facility in Djibouti, providing Beijing with far greater capacity to sustain its presence and build on its developments across the Indian Ocean. A quick review of trade partners for Indian Ocean littoral nations from the eastern coast of Africa, the island nations, and Australia and Indonesia, reveals Beijing as an important and key trading partner for the entire region. For example, for South Africa, Kenya, Tanzania, Madagascar, Yemen, Saudi Arabia, the UAE, Iran, Pakistan, India, Myanmar, Indonesia, and Australia—encompassing the entire Indian Ocean—China is the top import partner and a key trading partner.[33] Among the island nations, China is the top import partner for Sri Lanka, the Maldives, Mauritius, and Madagascar, and second for Comoros. The only nation in the Indian Ocean rim in which China is not among the top five trading partners, either in import or export, is Seychelles.[34]

Today, China has established itself as an important trading partner not only for the littoral and island nations of the Indian Ocean but also for key players such as India and Australia. China captured a moment in history where traditional and legacy players left an economic vacuum in the Indian Ocean and in their engagements with countries in the region. Given the scale and scope of China's economic engagements, Indian Ocean nations have welcomed Beijing's investments as a productive addition, and at times and alternative, to reliance on one key partner. Following the popular saying, "The flag follows trade," it is inevitable that China's flag (military) will follow its trade (economics) in the Indian Ocean. This in turn is beginning to change the geopolitical and military reality of the Indian Ocean in the broader context of growing US–China and India–China competition, tensions over the Taiwan Strait, military build-up in the South China Sea, and growing engagements from the South Pacific to Africa and Europe.

An Indian Ocean strategy

At the end of the Cold War, India, France, the US, and the UK emerged as the key players in the Indian Ocean. Both the UK and France, as former colonial powers, retained and maintained territories while also building bilateral partnerships with newly independent nations, albeit at different levels. The US increased its presence through the Cold War in its competition with the USSR, and India quickly emerged as a critical player in Indian Ocean geopolitics, taking on a strong multilateral role among newly independent nations through dominant foreign policies of that era such as those expressed by the Non-Aligned Movement (NAM). India's engagements in its neighborhood as well as with nations such as Mauritius established Delhi as a rising player. The US and USSR also played key roles in Indian Ocean developments such as the Sino-Indian War of 1962 and the Indo-Pakistani War of 1971 that led to an independent Bangladesh. Over time, Delhi established itself as an important rising political and security player in the region.

After the Cold War, the attention of these key players shifted in different directions. The US redirected its Indian Ocean presence toward sub-regional continental challenges, including the Gulf Wars and the war in Afghanistan. The Indian Ocean in effect turned into a transit route between the 5th fleet based in Bahrain and the 7th fleet in the Pacific Ocean. France continued its engagements with a focus on the Africa and the Middle East, emerging as the key player in the western Indian Ocean. The UK, as a legacy player, also continued to interact and engage with its partners and players, but its security commitments reduced significantly. The drawdown after the with-drawal from the east of Suez left London with limited capacity to develop and build on new initiatives. Moreover, America's wars in Afghanistan and the Middle East also saw British commitments drawn away from the maritime domain, as a key ally for Washington. India, for its part, focused on both its own internal development and the immediate neighborhood, began to play a more active role in the eastern Indian Ocean, around the South Asian neighborhood. As such, the Indian Ocean developed two distinct theaters of geopoli-tics: the western Indian Ocean with France playing an active role and the eastern Indian Ocean, with India assuming a central role.

As Washington moved from the Asia-Pacific to the Indo-Pacific beginning in 2017, the Indian Ocean was integrated within the Indo-Pacific strategy, but only nominally. However, the tendencies of the post-Cold War era remain present in much of the world's under-standing of the Indo-Pacific, shaped by a narrative set by Washington as an important global power. The primary focus for the US, as geog-raphy would dictate, remains the Pacific. The US had no specific Indian Ocean strategy as of early 2023. Since the region is divided into the three combatant commands mentioned, there is no nodal point in either the Department of State or Defense that assesses regional devel-opments in their entirety. The US Indo-Pacific strategy falls short of covering the Indian Ocean, which is a geographic theater that falls outside of its combatant commands. Diego Garcia, home to the only US base in the Indian Ocean, as Washington defines the region, is embroiled in a sovereignty dispute mired in British colonial history.[35] The absence of US maritime forces in the region,[36] outside of its conflicts in Afghanistan and the Middle East, has rendered Washington the absent power, post the Cold War. Today, Beijing can be viewed as the more engaged and present power in the region, whether measured through diplomatic missions or high-level visits, than the US across the Indian Ocean, from the Maldives to Comoros and Kenya to Saudi Arabia. China is also the welcomed power in the region, diplomatically, economically, and militarily, primarily due to its continued diplomatic engagements and growing economic investments.

Much of US strategy for the Indian Ocean focuses on India. For decades, Washington has argued for a more active Indian presence across the Indian Ocean, supporting Delhi's role as a net security provider. However, as the least funded service of the Indian Armed Forces, the Indian Navy has serious capacity constraints in sustaining a continuous presence across the wider Indian Ocean. The vast ocean, and its many strategically important sub-regions and chokepoints, require partners and friends to truly understand and address new challenges in the Indian Ocean. A partnership Washington under-utilizes in the Indian Ocean is that with France. With territories and presence across the Indian Ocean, and especially the western Indian Ocean, Paris is an important Indian Ocean player and can be a credible partner for Washington. A continental and geographic silo view of France, through the Atlantic lens, could explain why this mari-time partnership has not been unexplored. On the other hand, France is one of the most important maritime partners for New Delhi. Together with Australia, with a coast and islands in the Indian Ocean, the India–Australia–France trilateral has the potential to be a critical partnership for the region's geopolitical developments. While the announcement of AUKUS in 2021 created some fractures in the France–Australia relationship, both Canberra and Paris are on track to revive their relationship given the convergences in interests and priorities in both the Indian and Pacific oceans. While the UK is a natural player in the region—especially given that the Indian Ocean at one point was referred to as the "British Lake"[37]—its presence has been limited since London withdrew its forces east of Suez in early 1970s.

Regardless, all players will first have to study and assess the impor-tance of the Indian Ocean as one continuous theater before outsourcing the protection of their interests to partners and allies. As demonstrated through developments in the Solomon Islands, Sri

Lanka, and the Maldives, the maritime domain is complex and geopolitical developments of the twenty-first century differ significantly from those from the last century. As of early 2023, China has deployed naval ships and submarines, and established a base in Djibouti; it has strong partnerships with many of the littorals through military sales and is the only country with an embassy in each of the six island nations in the Indian Ocean: Sri Lanka, the Maldives, Mauritius, Seychelles, Madagascar, and Comoros. China today has a strong partnership with each of the sub-regions of the Indian Ocean through diplomatic, military, political, and economic ties, whether with African nations, the Middle East, or South Asia. Yet to be deployed is an aircraft carrier, which could possibly have happened by the time of the publication of this book or in the same year. Most importantly, China is beginning to offer solutions and invest in the region coherently, as one theater, through efforts such as the China–Indian Ocean Region Forum, established in 2022.

China is a welcomed player in the Indian Ocean, and a new component of Beijing's presence there will be supported by the western Indian Ocean and the island nations of the region—the two missing pieces in the geopolitical conversation about the Indian Ocean. While the western Indian Ocean is geographically excluded from national outreach in the Indian Ocean by players such as the US and Australia, the role of island nations in shaping great power competition is a new phenomenon. The next chapter details the rise of these sovereign nations and their role in great power competition, the swing states of the twenty-first century.

4

Island Nations' Agency and Great Power Competition

Island nations are vulnerable but not powerless.

Abdulla Shahid[1]

As underlined in the previous chapter, the Indian Ocean came to be viewed as divided into the eastern Indian Ocean and western Indian Ocean, with India and France emerging as key players. This was due to several factors, from the emergence of newly independent nations to Cold War rivalry to Washington's shifting priorities in continental Asia and the Middle East in the early 1990s. As many nations gained independence from France and the UK, Paris retained an interest in, and emerged as a key player for, nations on the eastern coast of Africa and island nations. Many of the island nations—Mauritius, Seychelles, Madagascar, and Comoros—are also French-speaking or have French as the official language. On the other hand, Sri Lanka and the Maldives were viewed as part of South Asia, where Delhi began to emerge as a key player. This division of the Indian Ocean was further accentuated after the Cold War and as island nations across the ocean gained independence. While the United States and the USSR remained the key big players across the ocean, competing with each other for access and influence, India and France emerged as two players in the eastern Indian Ocean and the western Indian Ocean respectively. Given that there is no actual division of the Indian Ocean, governments across the world came up with their own definitions and classifications of the Indian Ocean into different bureaus and departments.[2] As such, the island nations of the Indian Ocean region came to be divided as per the continents they were categorized as part of. The eastern Indian Ocean included Sri Lanka, the Maldives, India, Pakistan, Myanmar, and the Strait of Malacca, including the Andaman Sea. The French-speaking island nations of Mauritius, Seychelles, Madagascar, and Comoros, along with the coastal nations of eastern Africa, comprise much of the western Indian Ocean. The waters around the Bab-el-Mandeb and Strait of Hormuz, as well as the Persian Gulf and the Arabian Sea, constitute a sub-region of the northern and northwestern Indian Ocean, more commonly referred to as the Persian Gulf area. The southern Indian Ocean comprises mostly island territories of South Africa, France, and Australia. In effect, the islands that once were key to controlling the different points of the Indian Ocean were divided between Africa and South Asia, thereby reducing the importance of the maritime element in their identity, interactions, and geopolitics while advancing the continentalization of maritime issues. As the United States and USSR competed through the Cold War period, and France and India continued their engagements in the eastern and western Indian Ocean, there was little space for the island nations as these newly independent nations found themselves entangled in the increasingly continental-oriented geopolitics of the day. Bigger players and, more importantly, bigger neighbors, to an extent shaped the security environment where island nations found themselves balancing and navigating their own concerns among the priorities of their key strategic partners, France, India, and the US.

The geography of the island nations and their strategic importance, however, never diminished. What changed was the absence

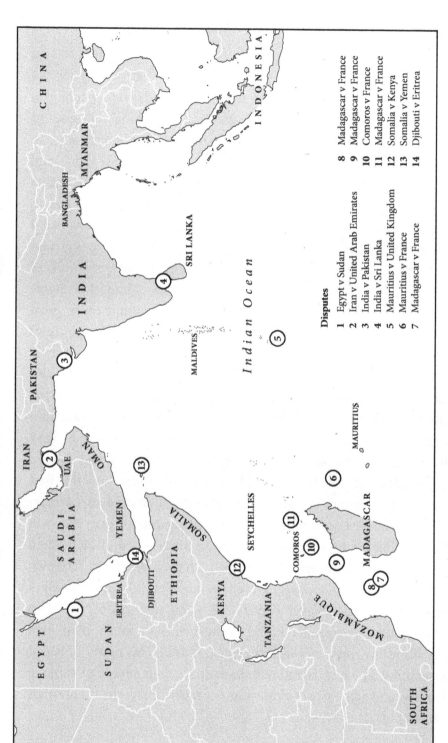

Map 4. Island sovereignty disputes in the Indian Ocean.

of direct competition. Particularly after the Cold War there was no active competition between powers in the Indian Ocean region, which pushed the importance of these islands and their geography to the periphery of great power competition. As China continues to emerge as a new political player and an important economic actor in the Indian Ocean, traditional players such as the US, India, and France find themselves, for the first time, competing with a nation that has no territories and a limited presence in the Indian Ocean. This is perhaps the first time that island agency has had a direct impact on great power competition, which is to say that great powers today must be aware of and study the sovereign choices exercised by island nations, and how these choices impact geopolitical conversations across the region. A key phenomenon of great power competition in the twenty-first century is the emergence of island nations as players in the geopolitical conversation—a new dynamic which carries its own set of implications. Geography and island agency take center stage within this subset of maritime competition today. Historically, bigger players did not have to take into consideration the choices of islands and island nations, as they were colonies unable to exercise sovereign rights or had limited engagement as newly independent nations. Today, for the first time, island nations are in a position where their choices, partnerships, priorities, commitments, and engagements can and will have a direct impact on how great powers interact with each other. Today, islands' geography, combined with their sovereign interests, has the power to shape great power narratives, unlike in any competition in the past. Bigger players are being and will be forced to re-evaluate and consider island engagements to secure their own maritime environments and strategic interests. This power of island geography, in which island nations exercise their sovereign choices, is a new and a key aspect of maritime competition in the twenty-first century.

The Indian Ocean and the island nations post-Cold War

Islands have always played an important role in great power competition. While islands always had to consider how their bigger powers and neighbors were interacting with each other, bigger players rarely had to think about the role islands play in their own competition. Mostly this was because islands were usually colonies or overseas bases up until the last time there was a great power competition between two superpowers or competing powers. Beyond the colonial period and after 1945, when the United States and the USSR competed for power and influence across different regions, many islands were still colonies of European powers and only beginning to gain their independence. This is true for the Indian Ocean region. However today, as the US and China compete for similar power and influence across the Indo-Pacific, and in particular in the Indian Ocean region, sovereign island nations are sitting across key communication and trading routes that hold the same geographic significance they did historically through different naval campaigns and wars.

After the end of the Cold War, as all the island nations in the Indian Ocean—Sri Lanka, the Maldives, Mauritius, Seychelles, Madagascar, and Comoros—became independent, the ocean moved from being a theater for great power competition to one with two dominant regional players, France and India. The US remained a key presence in the Indian Ocean but its focus turned primarily to continental challenges and interests in the Middle East and Afghanistan. Over time, the US maritime forces reduced the Indian Ocean to a transit route between its fleets in Tokyo and Bahrain.[3] Simultaneously, India and France emerged as two key players in the eastern and western Indian Ocean respectively. Delhi assumed a growing maritime role, led by its navy in the northern and eastern Indian Ocean, while France remained a key player for the southwest and western Indian Ocean. The island nations of the region were divided by the players into their own spheres of influence, with Sri Lanka and the Maldives forging closer ties with India, and Madagascar and Comoros with France. Mauritius and Seychelles developed close relationships equally with India and western players, including former colonial powers such as France and the UK. Given that Mauritius, Seychelles, Madagascar, and Comoros are all French-speaking, France emerged as the key partner for the African islands in the Indian Ocean. However, diaspora played a significant role in forging deep ties between the island of Mauritius and India. This close partnership exists today, with shared commonalities on commitments such as decolonization. Island nations as sovereign players sought to develop and expand their partnerships—economic, military, diplomatic, and political—and India and France assumed their positions as security providers in the region. Economic and diplomatic engagements developed parallel to military engagements. Through the 1980s and 1990s, island nations were also undergoing their own tremendous domestic developments, for example the civil war in Sri Lanka, a military coup in the Maldives, and unrest and protest as leaders of these nations worked toward bringing different ethnic groups under the flag and boundary of one nation after centuries of colonial rule. Much like any nation emerging from centuries of colonial rule, island nations too went through their own historical shifts and transformations, in search of their own identity, integration, and place in global affairs as a new nation. Each island nation has its own significant history, shaped by their environment and political identity, and it is worth understanding each of these histories. For instance, Sri Lanka, the Maldives, Mauritius, and Seychelles gained independence from the UK in 1948, 1965, 1968, and 1976 respectively. Madagascar and Comoros gained independence from France in 1960 and 1975. As is evident, many of the island nations only gained independence well after the onset of the Cold War, which greatly shaped their security environment in their early years of independence. The Indian Navy largely took on the role exercised by the British Royal Navy as London began to withdraw its forces from the region. This was true especially for Sri Lanka and the

Table 2. Military and economic partners of the island nations of the Indian Ocean.

Western Indian Ocean

Country	Military partners	Top import partners	Top export partners
Madagascar	UAE	1. China 2. France 3. India 4. UAE 5. South Africa	1. United States 2. France 3. UAE 4. Germany 5. China
Comoros	NA	1. UAE 2. China 3. France 4. Pakistan 5. India	1. India 2. Greece 3. France 4. Germany 5. Türkiye
Seychelles	India	1. UAE 2. BVI 3. Germany 4. Cayman Islands 5. Belize	1. Bermuda 2. France 3. Cayman Islands 4. United Kingdom 5. Japan
Mauritius	India	1. China 2. UAE 3. India 4. France 5. South Africa	1. France 2. United States 3. South Africa 4. United Kingdom 5. Zimbabwe

Eastern Indian Ocean

Country	Military partners	Top import partners	Top export partners
Sri Lanka	India United States	1. China 2. India 3. UAE 4. Malaysia 5. Singapore	1. United States 2. United Kingdom 3. India 4. Germany 5. Italy
Maldives	India	1. China 2. India 3. UAE 4. Singapore 5. Sri Lanka	1. Thailand 2. France 3. Germany 4. India 5. United States

Maldives, even though British military forces maintained some presence even after independence. Finally, outside of Diego Garcia, British forces had left most places and bases in the Indian Ocean, maintaining a footprint in some areas in accordance with Britain's alliance with the US and the priorities of the time, mainly in the Asian/Iranian side of the Persian Gulf. However, the political history of the island nations is outside the scope of this book and the following sections of the chapter focus primarily on the islands in terms of their maritime identity and their role in great power competition.

As island nations struggled through their internal turmoil to unify their nations and people under their new sovereign identity, political leaders from islands turned to their bigger neighbors (in terms of their size and military capability in particular) for stability, security, and growth. Where the island nations viewed this as a form of new bilateral relationship, bigger nations—especially India and France—assumed a more permanent role, becoming their key security partners. In this process of island nations clarifying their identity, and their endeavor to find international partners, these traditional players in the Indian Ocean became complacent in their position as important partners for island nations, which naturally carried an underlying strategic interest.

This balance of power, with India assuming a greater role in the eastern Indian Ocean and France in the western Indian Ocean, and with the US as the global power in the region, continued unchallenged after the Cold War and well into the early 2010s, although the sub-regional dynamics had come into play through the 1960s and the Cold War period. The three powers learned accept each other's place and position in the Indian Ocean, with changing dynamics and hostility among the players themselves, such Washington's support toward Pakistan, during the Indo-Pakistani War of 1971,[4] leading to the independence of Bangladesh. On the other hand, Delhi and Paris forged stronger ties politically and strategically. Both nations also shared a common interest in maintaining stability in the Indian

Ocean and securing their roles as key players in the region.[5] India and France today also share a major defense partnership, with Paris being one of Delhi's most strategic and important maritime partners. Washington, for its part, continued to encourage Delhi to assume a greater role in the Indian Ocean so as to address its own challenges in terms of capacity following its wars in Afghanistan and the Middle East.

In the wider geopolitical conversation, the developments within the territorial boundaries of island nations came to be viewed through the lens of their impact on maritime security across sea lines of communication and any resulting changes in the strategic reality of the Indian Ocean. The new players in the Indian Ocean, engaged in managing their own geopolitical developments of the post-Cold War period, failed to recognize and understand the agency of island sovereignties and their impact on shaping great power competition. The unchallenged emergence of France and India as the security providers in the region led to strategic inertia and a diplomatic stand-still in engaging with the island nations of the Indian Ocean. There is an argument to be made that often it was island nations that sought support from bigger powers and neighbors to address evolving security issues within their territories and environment.[6] While island nations viewed this as a request for support from key partners, it is likely bigger powers assumed that their role as security providers for small island nations across the Indian Ocean made them indispensable. Paris, Washington, and Delhi perhaps assumed there would be no challenge to their role as security providers, failing to see the evolution of islands' agency as sovereign nations and the role it would come to play in shaping great power competition in the twenty-first century.

As the region grapples with competition between India and China in the Indian Ocean and China and the US at a more global level, it should be noted that island agency has very much paved the way for China's emergence in the Indian Ocean, which has been welcomed by the island nations of the Indian Ocean. This was a direct result of maritime security being pushed to the periphery of geopolitical conversations and engagements in the latter half of the twentieth and first decade of the twenty-first century. As we continue to work on understanding the impact of great power competition in the Indian Ocean today, it is important to recognize, acknowledge, and listen to the needs, voices, and challenges of island nations of the Indian Ocean.[7]

Debt-trap or welcome investments?

The Hambantota port in Sri Lanka is perhaps the best-known contemporary development reflecting the factors shaping the new dynamics of the Indian Ocean. The Chinese Belt and Road Initiative[8] which includes the Maritime Silk Road (MSR)[9] is widely considered as an extension of China's interest in the Indian Ocean region. The MSR is the maritime aspect of Beijing's Belt and Road Initiative, which aims to connect China to Europe through the Indian Ocean. Launched in 2013, it envisions promoting greater maritime connectivity by building ports and maritime infrastructure along the MSR route. It is often discussed[10] as the project that aims to offer China strategic and military advantages in the maritime domain, allowing it to build on its existing investments, interactions, and presence through this region.

The geostrategic implications of the MSR are perhaps most evident through its projects in Sri Lanka, Pakistan, and Myanmar, in particular the Hambantota port in Sri Lanka. The port, constructed with assistance from Chinese loans, came to be viewed as Beijing's ploy to create investments in key ports across the Indo-Pacific, which could be turned into strategic or military gains. The narrative unfolded as China leveraged its economic heft as a way of tricking unsuspecting nations into agreements which were economically unfeasible from the start. When nations fail to meet repayments related to loans and aid for development projects, Beijing will strike a deal where China gets access to a strategic port in exchange for delayed or unmet payments. As one *New York Times* report notes regarding the developments over the Hambantota port: "The case is one of the most vivid examples of China's ambitious use of loans and aid to gain influence around the world—and of its willingness to play hardball to collect."[11]

The argument that China aims to use its economic engagement for strategic and military purposes is not unfounded. However, the perceptions of traditional players gave far too much credit to Beijing for a grand strategy crafted by China to create a string of ports and bases across the Indian Ocean, without taking into consideration the maritime dynamics at play today. This approach, of using trade and economic engagements to expand military or strategic interests, is not new. Flag follows trade, it always does, and as colonial history should have taught us, military interests will continue to follow the commercial interests of a nation and provide security. It is one of the core priorities and missions of a navy. Beijing is perhaps following strategies and tradecraft employed by Imperial Japan and the British empire. Both relied a great deal on access to key bases and ports, following economic interests in establishing dominance across vast oceans and seas. The difference in the twenty-first century, however, is that these projects are equally welcomed by and at times sought by the host nations to begin with. In Sri Lanka's Hambantota example, or in the Maldives' China friendship bridge, conversations with officials in Colombo and Malé will clarify that Beijing was the final stop in their objective to fund these projects. The initial conversation is usually with strategic partners, in this case India, as well as Japan, which emerged as a key development assistance partner for most Indian Ocean nations after World War II. While Beijing, in my view, is pursuing a strategy and following an ambition to better connect its coast to those in the Indian Ocean and Europe, a key aspect of this narrative is the role that island nations are playing in advancing this objective. Great power conversations often happen among great powers or nations who view others as their equals. As Beijing undertook its ambitious MSR project, most nations failed to take into consideration the role island agency would play in shaping and framing the implications of such a project. So a question of equal importance for traditional players is, why did island nations turn to China for their development projects, despite their strong partnerships with key traditional players? This goes back to the argument earlier in the chapter as to how traditional players entered a stage of strategic inertia in their engagements with island nations. Combined with the power of island agency in the twenty-first century, and China's ready capital, initiative, and willingness to invest in infrastructure projects, the strategic reality of Indian Ocean geopolitics rapidly began to shift. Although traditional players have now regained an active engagement strategy with island nations both in the Indian and Pacific oceans, the world will need to accommodate a new kind of great power competition, where island nations and small states can and will impact great power interactions in the twenty-first century, a phenomenon unseen in past great power competitions.

Regarding Beijing, the conversation is less about good and bad power, and more about power itself. Nations with great power ambitions, when empowered by economic and military strength, behave the same way. The competition this time around is different because it is taking place after the end of the colonial period, within the norms of the United Nations and existing treaties and conventions, customs, and codes of conduct. China's rise and approach toward its road to being a global player is shaped by those who came before Beijing, at least in the maritime domain. While the approach from Beijing may be similar to those of historical naval powers, such as the British Navy or the Imperial Japanese Navy, contextualized by the postcolonial word, the response would have to be completely different. In essence, traditional players will have to find a new answer to an old problem, situated within the norms of the twenty-first century.

On the question of debt-trap diplomacy,[12] the idea that Beijing has a grand strategy to trap smaller nations into unsustainable loans and grants, resulting in the receiving nations going into debt and the nations being entrapped by Chinese intentions, again fails to recognize island agency. Many of the projects identified as markers of China's debt-trap diplomacy, such as those in Sri Lanka or Pakistan, were implemented at the request of the host nations. Of course, there is an element of intensive diplomatic and economic outreach from Beijing, but the projects were still ideas that emerged from the debt-trapped nation in question.[13] The choice to partner with Beijing is also a reflection of fraught relations between island nations and their traditional security partners, as well as the island nations' desire to expand their partnerships. There has been research debunking the debt-trap diplomacy myth,[14] but the Hambantota case, which resulted in Beijing gaining access to the port for 99 years, set a strong narrative and example of what China is seeking to do in the Indian Ocean. In reality, this was indeed a sharp reminder of the emerging competition between China and the traditional security providers of island nations. Delhi in particular was caught off guard, with many of its neighbors, from Nepal, Bangladesh, and Sri Lanka to the Maldives, entering into deep and intensifying economic, political, and military engagements with China. The tendency to perceive regional developments through the lens of the bigger power meant that most nations, including India, failed to understand and recognize the role islands had begun to play in shaping great power competition. While there was a recognition that China's intensifying engagements with India's neighbors were aimed at minimizing Delhi's influence in the region, there was a lesser understanding of Beijing's interests in advancing its partnership with island nations to advance its wider and larger maritime goals, irrespective of India's preferences. India, France, the US, Australia, Japan, and others began their own initiatives bilaterally and collectively—such as Delhi and Tokyo's Asia Africa growth corridor, or Japan's partnership for quality infrastructure—to both counter and balance Chinese infrastructure projects, yet failed to study, examine, and understand the sentiments on the ground in island nations as well as islands' agency. To Delhi, Tokyo, and others, the answer was simply: they must find ways to counter China's charm offensive by launching their own initiatives. These policies were reactive and rested entirely on the interaction with China. However, to really understand these developments and the changing dynamics of the region, we have to flip the narrative to understand the island perspective. Great power competition reduced the role of islands to the theater for competition, but islands in the era of the Indo-Pacific are reclaiming both their island identity and their agency to affect change and competition.

The island view[15]

A key question to deliberate with regard to geopolitics of the Indian Ocean today is whether China really is a new player in the region. At the moment, in 2023, China is the only nation with an embassy in each of the islands of the Indian Ocean, and many of these diplomatic missions date back to the 1950s and 1960s. Sri Lanka was the first country from South Asia to give "diplomatic recognition" to the PRC in 1950[16] and China was the first nation to recognize Comorian independence from France.[17]

A series of interviews and closed-door conversations in Colombo, Malé, Port Louis, Antananarivo, and Moroni (in Sri Lanka, the Maldives, Mauritius, Madagascar, and Comoros respectively) helped with understanding the island perspective and view on the Indian Ocean and maritime security. Often the narrative on geopolitics is set by the tone of bigger players, and the island view somewhat dismissed or undermined. There is also a tendency to work with smaller nations through an approach geared toward "helping" small nations better understand and manage their own security challenges, as though they are unaware of the security challenges facing their own countries. The conversations on the ground underlined a deep-seated frustration with India, France, the US, and the UK in particular, and their strategic arrogance. The common themes that emerged from these conversations were centered on the importance of island identity and sovereignty (that islands won't swap their territory for infrastructure projects), the desire to expand their partnerships, and the differences in the concept of security between island nations and their security partners. The next sections of this chapter are a concerted effort to provide a unilateral view of how islands perceive geopolitics and recent developments (based on first-hand interviews), given that their perspective continues to remain at the periphery of geopolitics of great power competition today. The island view can be divided into two sub-categories: perspectives on geopolitics and defining maritime security for an island nation.

Geopolitics

As China's MSR gained traction across the globe and the narrative on debt-trap diplomacy became a popularly accepted conversation, most officials on island nations would begin the conversations by underlining the importance of sovereignty and independence. There is a growing recognition that Beijing is filling a "void" that emerged from the strategic inertia of traditional partners. Recent developments, particularly between 2015 and 2018 in both Sri Lanka and the Maldives, where governments in the island nations took on a strong anti-India and pro-China stance,[18] underline the desire to expand beyond traditional partners. As conversations in Malé would underline, "[Abdulla] Yameen taught you [India] a great lesson—what can happen if you are not paying attention."[19] Abdulla Yameen Abdul Gayoom is a Maldivian politician who was the president of the island country between 2013 and 2018. Yameen's term was rife with controversies and is viewed as an administration that advanced the Maldives' partnership with China, causing friction and discomfort with and in India. Under Yameen's presidency, the Maldives saw a political crisis in 2018, with the imprisonment of political opposition figures in the island nation. This crisis accentuated the Sino-Indian competition in the Indian Ocean, where both Delhi and Beijing stood to play a part, should there be interest.[20] This was also an indication of Beijing's increasing presence and ability to sustain itself in the eastern Indian Ocean, and to offer support and assistance, should a partner request it. In Indian Ocean dynamics, this crisis considerably shifted the geopolitics of the Indian Ocean, with the US and India on one side and China on the other.

As a result, in Malé's view, Delhi doubled down on its intention to remain the key partner for the Maldives, limiting its partnership with other players. Malé views China and India as the main players, but the Maldives government of President Ibrahim Solih (who came to power after the 2018 political crisis) adopted an "India first" foreign policy to underscore Delhi's importance in the evolving Sino-Indian competition. However, officials warned against viewing the Maldives' "India first" policy in literal terms, stating that "India first does not mean India only."[21] From an island point of view, this means giving consideration to Indian sensitivities, recognizing India as the closest neighbor and generator of security in the Indian Ocean region, and as first responders. Elaborating on the difficult position of being caught in the competition between two of its major partners, interviews in Malé underscored the following: "The India first policy is sometimes misunderstood. What we mean is we will always be mindful of India's legitimate security concerns. We will not take foreign policy decisions that will threaten India's security. It doesn't mean our other relationships are secondary." Malé underlines its long-standing ties with China despite its partnership with India, but the government under Yameen took a conscious decision to prioritize its partnership with China. Officials recognized that would make India uncomfortable given the dynamics between Beijing and New Delhi. Given the long-standing political and military history between India and the Maldives, the latter's increased and deepening partnership with China, a nation India has been at war with, is viewed in India as a political betrayal. In India's view, Delhi has offered support and assistance to Malé throughout its history and that warrants a careful consideration of engagements with India's rivals. The worsening political relationship between India and China, primarily due to its continental border dispute along India's north and northeastern borders, accentuates this competition in the Indian Ocean. Islands also articulate that they do not seek to play one player off against another, and that there are historical ties with each of the major players. However, they also understand the need to balance players and their investments in the island nations and the need to cooperate with all development partners. The Maldives recognizes the importance of its partnership with India but doesn't want to pursue it at the cost of its relationship with China. Delhi certainly is the first responder for the Maldives, given its geography, but this does not diminish Beijing's extension of help and aid in Malé's view. The core island perspective on geopolitics is to maintain independence and sovereignty which, from an island point of view, can only be maintained through multiple equally important partnerships and reducing dependency on any one country. Officials in Malé under-scored this important point by noting that the Maldives' security relies on partnerships far and wide. Multilateral engagements and partnerships provide comfort and security to the Maldives and prevent the nation being over-reliant on any one nation. "We don't want to become a threat to anybody or anyone, but we also don't want to be threatened. Our main aim is to protect our sovereignty."[22]

Conversations in Port Louis underlined similar sentiments, where India, China, France, and the UK are all important players. As per views from Mauritius, "Small islands have no choice but to foster strategic partnerships" to balance bigger players' interests around their waters. Islands don't fear invasion; the concept of security is geared more toward protection, and primarily the protection of their vast Exclusive Economic Zones (EEZs). On the growing discontent toward traditional partners across island nations, officials in Mauritius underlined a disconnect. In an effort to capture the issue in an example, one official noted "the days of *tabla* diplomacy are over."[23] This apparently points toward a practice on the part of Indian high commissioners posted to Mauritius, who would bring *tablas*, Indian hand drums, and distribute them among the locals in villages. At a more nuanced level, that sentiment meant to underpin two shifts, first, that a strong Indian diaspora does not mean that Indian-origin Mauritians have the same affinity to India as Indians do, and, second, that culture is a connecting bridge, not a tool to enforce a sense of loyalty. In essence, the message was that it is no longer enough to extend cultural diplomacy or continue with efforts that worked four decades earlier. The geopolitics has changed, as has the competition, along with Mauritians' strong sense of identity as islanders and Mauritians first, and everything else second. Underlining such sentiments among the younger population of the island, officials emphasized the dismissal of diplomatic protocols on the part of traditional players. At a press conference regarding a new metro project in Mauritius with investments from India, the then Indian high commissioner was apparently sitting with the Mauritian prime minister, which was noted as "very undiplomatic." More than protocol, it inadvertently translates into disrespect toward a sovereign nation, where Delhi fails to extend basic and minimum diplomatic courtesy, which islands feels stem from India's assumptions about its role as a key player in the Indian Ocean. In contrast, Beijing is seen as conducting its business quietly, without attracting much attention. This does not mean that Port Louis seeks to forge closer relationships with other players in an effort to replace Delhi.

The above developments capture the mood of small island nations and their view on how they are treated by their closest security partners. For Port Louis, Delhi remains a key military, strategic, and economic partner, including in building strategic port infrastructures such as on the Agaléga islands. One of these strategically located Mauritian islands has been rumored to be an Indian military base, based on images that show an airstrip and jetty among other infrastructure development.[24] A 2021 report by *Al Jazeera* points toward Delhi's hidden agenda of quietly turning the port into a military facility. As per interviews in 2017, officials in Mauritius's Prime Minister's Office, and the National Security Advisor's office, were pointing toward productive development of the India–Mauritius relationship in initiating projects such as Agaléga, which, at the time of the interviews (2017), was scheduled to begin the following year. Underlining the need for such development—which echoes similar concerns in the Maldives and other islands in the Indian Ocean—officials point toward capacity to manage, monitor, and deliver services to outlying islands of the nation. As per interviews in 2017 (years before the much-cited *Al Jazeera* investigative article), the Indian Navy plays a key role in monitoring and securing Mauritius's EEZ. It is widely known that Delhi deploys its surveillance aircraft twice a year to Mauritius and Seychelles in support of the island nations' Maritime Domain Awareness (MDA) efforts. The new infrastructure on Agaléga is built with the aim of providing services to the local population on the island, as well as supporting military efforts in increasing island nations' MDA capabilities. Emphasizing the need for such developments, officials on the islands note, "There are 250 people on Agaléga; there are no jetties, you have to drop anchor. It takes 44 hours to reach Agaléga by ship, it takes five hours on Donier aircraft."[25] The extension of the jetty, airstrip, and its associated developments, as per the officials on the island, is designed both to provide services to the local population and to bolster existing collaboration with India on EEZ patrols. That the island and the new facilities could be used by Indian naval assets in undertaking its activities is very much a possibility. If that does happen, it will certainly be a product of bilateral discussion between Port Louis and Delhi, a development which is more likely today than in 2017, given the dramatic shift in Indian

Ocean geopolitics between China and India. It is the competition with China, and caution over building ports for military gains, which has led to a tussle between opposing political parties, each accusing of the other of selling strategic land to either India or China.[26]

There are, however, strong sentiments on the subject in Mauritius—about local people losing their homes on strategic islands due to the military interests of bigger nations. The fate of Diego Garcia and the Chagossians at the time Mauritius became independent is a cautionary and personal tale for many on the island. The current fate of the islands remains in question. The initial agreement on Chagos, which was for a period of 50 years, is over, and Port Louis has demanded the islands back as its sovereign territory. This has been met with disregard by the US and UK, leaving an even deeper fear of the consequences of great power competition on island sovereignty. Despite Mauritius's repeated victories at the International Court of Justice (ICJ) and support for Mauritius at the UN General Assembly, London for several years refused to discuss the matter with Port Louis, automatically renewing its agreement with Washington to lease the island base for another 20 years.[27] Senior officials from the islands have come out publicly on multiple occasions to say that Washington can retain the base as Port Louis recognizes the importance of the facility in maintaining security across the Indian Ocean. However, this is a case of sovereignty, and respecting rules and norms as established within the UN Charter, and Port Louis believes London must acknowledge its claim and return the islands to Mauritius.[28] With a new government in London in September 2022, the UK has now agreed to consult and enter conversation with Mauritius to discuss the issue of Diego Garcia, which has been an ongoing effort. These experiences continue to shape the perspectives, views, and concerns of small island nations, and their emphasis on the importance of sovereignty and island agency.

The emphasis on sovereignty as a security challenge for small islands reappeared in all the author's conversations across the Indian Ocean. In Moroni, in 2019, officials underlined that "the main national security challenge for Comoros is security and sovereignty."[29] Similar to other island nations in the western Indian Ocean, Comoros too had a background of being a new nation coming out of European colonialism, and faced the dilemma of being embroiled in a sovereignty dispute with the power it considered its primary security partner, in Moroni's case, France. To summarize the strategic islands' political partnerships and its position within the international community, Comoros identifies France, China, and Saudi Arabia as its main political partners. An African Muslim nation, Comoros considers itself the link between Africa and the Muslim world, an "open" (a word used repeatedly by nations across Indian Ocean islands to indicate that it welcomes partnerships from everyone) country, which has many opportunities for tourism but also requires assistance in development projects. The phrase that perhaps best captures Comoros's views and perspectives on the islands' security and development concerns would be: "France is both a first partner and a security challenge." Elaborating on the issue, every meeting in Moroni began with a description of the archipelagic nation, which consists of four islands—Grand Comore, Anjoun, Moheli, and Mayotte. Using strong words, officials refer to Mayotte as the island "stolen" by the French. Mayotte is a French overseas department and has held referendums in which the island voted to be part of French territory.[30] There appears to be great discontent among the Comorian government toward France, as both its primary partner and the source of many "troubles" for the island. From the perspective of Comoros, it is hard to compete with the benefits Mayotte residents would enjoy as citizens of France compared to those they would as citizens of Comoros. This, in turn, provides a disadvantageous position to Comoros, whereby Paris can continue justify jurisdiction over Mayotte through referendums, which is more a reflection of economic opportunity than the reality of a nation with strong colonial history with France. In Moroni's view, decisions within the European Union (EU) and in the western Indian Ocean, including on Comoros, are led by France. As France is one of the five permanent members of the UN Security Council, Comoros feels its options to resolve its territorial dispute are limited, as Paris (in Moroni's view) can veto any decision on Mayotte. In no uncertain terms, Comoros is actively seeking partners in an effort to balance French influence within its borders as well as in the immediate region. Officials also noted that Asian nations leave the western Indian Ocean to France, which in Moroni's view is a missed opportunity.

As French citizens and members of the EU, Mayotte residents have access to better conditions than the population of the union of Comoros. Officials recognize this and point toward an issue of immigration, where more of Comoros' own citizens are going to Mayotte because of the strength of the euro. It also creates another issue, that of becoming a transit point for drugs. In Moroni's view, this is enabled by Mayotte's access to the euro, giving its residents more purchasing power than those of its neighbors on the other three islands. As per interviews, in an effort to expand its commercial ties, Comoros seeks greater partnership with Gulf nations, as well as Morocco and Egypt. In Moroni's view, a second key partner of Comoros after France is Saudi Arabia, for both political and economic purposes.[31] However, as per the Economic Complexity Observatory (OEC) data for August 2022 to September 2023, China emerges as the top export partner for the island nation.[32]

The island deeply values its partnership with China, which appears to be the key nation outside of France, along with being the first country to establish an embassy in Comoros. Leaders greatly appreciated Beijing building roads, and the parliament for Comoros and noted, "we (Comoros) need more from China. We are in conversation with China on ports, roads, and airports."[33]

The island nation has made an assessment of the potential prospects of gas and petroleum being present in its sovereign waters: "The prospect of gas and petroleum around Comorian waters is very high, the waters are very deep, and Comoros wants to be able to explore the exact volume. Our assessment is that majority of petroleum gases on the site is toward Mozambique Channel and we are looking for international companies to help us make that assessment."[34] The island nation is seeking partnership on hydrographic missions. Comoros is an archipelagic country, however, and there is limited knowledge on the presence and the volumes of natural resources in its EEZ. Some discoveries of petrol, gas, and other resources have been made, particularly on the coast of the Mozambique Channel. The message was clear on setting security as a priority—security is connected to the sustainable use of the oceans. In elaborating the priorities for the nation, officials noted, "We recognize that our future is at sea, our development is tied to the sustainable harness of the oceans. Comoros needs training and help in capacity building like in the fishing industry—how to produce, process, store, transform. We need experience and training. We ask our partners to train us to handle disaster, to respond and to better manage, we want resilient infrastructure."[35]

Engaging in conversations across the island nations of the Indian Ocean was the most useful and effective tool to record and measure island perspectives, which allows for an examination and study of the factors driving new developments, dynamics, and competition in the Indian Ocean. While on the surface, the dominant narrative from the traditional powers is on the Belt and Road Initiative and the Maritime Silk Road as key tools for changing dynamics in the Indian Ocean, a view from the islands helps us understand that these are only one aspect of the conversation. Shifting sentiments in island nations, changing dynamics between islands and their key security partners, and the need for expanded partnerships are playing an equally significant role in shaping the geopolitics of the Indian Ocean region, and much of this is spurred on by island agency.

On maritime security

Maritime security is a broad term and is defined by a nation's outlook, priorities, and challenges in the maritime domain. For most bigger nations, maritime security first includes military threats, followed by non-military challenges emerging from the sea. For all island nations, maritime security comprises the following: Illegal, Unidentified, and Unregulated (IUU) fishing, climate change, drug trafficking, and human smuggling. For most islands, national security and defense issues are related to those areas. As Malé notes, IUU fishing, drug trafficking, climate vulnerability, and sea-level rise are the biggest national security concerns. With the Maldives placed at the center of the Indian Ocean, officials in Malé further noted that both opportunities and challenges arise from the sea and affect the island nation. Oil pollution and natural disasters are the other key areas of concern and matters of national security as these have significant repercussions for the economy, affecting tourism.

In the western Indian Ocean, for Mauritius and Seychelles, along with issues of climate and IUU fishing, drug smuggling is a dominant concern, as well as money laundering. In the view of the two islands, the drug trade moves toward Europe and for local consumption in eastern Africa. As destinations for luxury tourism, both Mauritius and Seychelles find themselves at the crossroads of the movement of drugs across the Indian Ocean. For the Indian Ocean Commission (IOC), the sub-regional forum consisting of islands in the western Indian Ocean—Mauritius, Seychelles, Madagascar, Comoros, and France (through the overseas department of La Réunion)—drug smuggling is a key concern.[36] The IOC is keen to develop better legal frameworks on trafficking, along with providing information and training to meet this challenge. On issues of security, the islands are of the view that it must be perceived holistically, as "one package," encompassing the economic, development, and security aspects. The islands recognize that their key partners divide security concerns into traditional and non-traditional security issues, providing only one point of view. However, in the islands' view, all is interconnected and one aspect is related to others. In developing better regulations and frameworks, the islands also recognize the challenges of connectivity among the islands themselves. Islands in the western Indian Ocean mentioned the "Vanilla airlines,"[37] a sub-regional initiative to promote better air connectivity among island nations, which has seen limited success. The name "Vanilla islands" refers to the five islands of the western Indian Ocean (also members of the IOC), which all grow vanilla and export vanilla products.

All islands underlined the importance of MDA, to better monitor and surveil its coastal waters and EEZ, to address issues of trafficking and smuggling. As coast guards from the region point out, island nations are focused on EEZ surveillance as the region has become a hub for drug trafficking and shipments. But the drugs are not coming from island EEZs, and there is limited capability to track and monitor the drug routes. Every nation, big or small, is unified in the assessment that no one country can fight maritime crimes alone, nor can MDA be achieved by any one nation. This mammoth task is only achievable through partnerships. On creating the right domain awareness, islands have further suggestions: "don't just give us the tools, give us the skills as well as the technology. Technology and skills go hand in hand . . . how do you detect the drugs? How are the bigger powers doing it?"[38] These are some issues for which island nations and maritime agencies seek assistance to help build their own capacity. In their view, there is an element of geopolitics which hinders progress and development in addressing maritime crime: "Geopolitics between India, China, UK, France, and the US is a major hindrance to letting the region come together."

Island nations, and Madagascar and Comoros in particular, raised the issue of oil pollution and the increase in corruption around issues such as fishing rights within their EEZ. Madagascar recognizes the challenges, in that its national security strategy has traditionally relied on French expertise, which it now believes is not entirely compatible with its own aims. "The goal now is to create Madagascar's own strategy in order to better manage the blue economy." Focusing on both the island nation's strategic location and the issue of oil pollution, the Malagasy Navy points toward the maritime route passing close to the island, which leads to issues such as oil spills created by big tankers. The Mozambique Channel is a key route for big oil tankers, which constitute almost "30% of global tanker traffic."[39] (See Map 3 for energy transit in the Indian Ocean.)

In Madagascar's view, this also creates issues of piracy in the Mozambique Channel, as well as bringing drugs to the Indian Ocean. Antananarivo also pointed toward the density of maritime traffic that passes near the southern border of the island nation, underlining the need for greater MDA capacity, as well as capabilities, for the islands. Madagascar and Mauritius are platforms for drugs and traffickers, while Seychelles is an endpoint among island dynamics. Asked what the Malagasy Navy's message would be to its international partners the reply was: "Fix all of these maritime and economic issues and help Madagascar—this is our message to the international community and to our friends and partners. Let's stop the problem in Madagascar to prevent it from traveling to other parts of the Indian Ocean."[40] The navy points to a lack of resources, assets, and technology, noting that Madagascar has no coastal radar, which is critical for generating MDA. It is worth pointing out that India has undertaken an initiative to provide radars to Indian Ocean islands in an effort to boost maritime security across the region. However, Madagascar and Comoros were left out of this Indian Ocean initiative, perhaps due to India's own division of the Indian Ocean into different categories of priorities.[41] However, Madagascar hosts the Regional Maritime Information Fusion Centre (RMIFC) under the IOC, funded by the European Commission,[42] with strong support from France. A fusion center's primary objective is to collate and analyze maritime information so as to detect illegal activities as well as identify maritime trends. This is a welcome effort in the region, but islands also underline the need to first strengthen national capacities so they can truly contribute toward international efforts such as the RMIFC.

Adding to Madagascar's identification of oil tankers and oil spills as an issue in the Mozambique Channel, Comoros also notes the impact on the environment. Big tankers drop litter which travels to the Comorian coast, impacting both environment and tourism. This again constitutes a national security challenge as it is connected to economic growth of the island. But small islands' voices are not considered a serious challenge as their bigger partners consider military threats as a priority for national security concerns. Comoros also underlines the impact of natural disasters, a common phenomenon in the Indian Ocean, to island security and economic growth. There is an immediate need for capacity and training to respond to humanitarian crises at sea as well as rehabilitation efforts post disaster.

If the island nations' navy and coast guard are tasked with addressing crises at sea, they must have the assets and capacity to be able to do so. In that, both Madagascar and Comoros note France's desire to monitor the island's waters, and that it is willing only to provide small second-hand boats. For second-hand assets, the cost of maintenance is higher, which traps the navy or coast guard in a loop of being reliant on the partner that provided the asset. For both Comoros and Madagascar, the goal is to acquire new ships at least 50 meters or more in length, which will provide the capability to stay at sea for longer periods of time. Both nations are actively seeking partners to meet this demand, recognizing the importance of growing their navy's ability to remain at sea if political leaders want to develop their blue economy.

Comoros clearly identifies five key areas as essential for its blue economy, which is linked to its growth.

1. A sea port for its military vessels, which is a defense priority.
2. Larger military vessels, a minimum of 50 meters long. This is important for patrolling and interception at sea, with repercussions for search and rescue.

3. Coastal radar for surveillance and information, including training and technical know-how.
4. Technology for tsunami and cyclone warning systems to alert civilians and secure them.
5. Capability to manage and mitigate disasters including for rehabilitation and reconstruction.

Although in this case articulated by Comoros, the five areas listed are common themes that emerged in most conversations across island nations in the Indian Ocean.

When discussed through the lens of great power competition, maritime security most often takes on a military perspective divided between traditional and non-traditional security issues. The islands, however, see these issues as more interconnected, as their geography and resources, and access to key waterways, place them at the crossroads of great power competition while managing challenges considered as "soft security" by their key partners. In the twenty-first century, with island nations regaining their place as key battlegrounds for competition and influence, it is important to remember their agency as sovereign nations and the impact this has on regional developments. It is no longer enough to study the actions and behaviors of great powers at sea and in foreign policy to examine and understand the metrics of geopolitics. Armed with their sovereign choices, sitting in key geographic locations, island nations for the first time have both the agency and ability to accelerate or reduce great power competition, significantly impacting regional dynamics. While conflicts will break out between powers with sizeable navies, the road to conflict, and much of the competition, will be over influence and access to small island nations, and forging partnerships with them. In doing so, traditional players in the Indian Ocean—India, France, the US, and the UK—need to review and revise their Indian Ocean policies to take into account the new sentiments, concerns, and priorities of the island nations. It is worth noting that while much of this has begun to make an impression in Delhi, Paris, Washington, and London, and among their friends in Canberra and Tokyo, traditional players will also have to manage and address legacy issues. While China is a problematic player in the western Indian Ocean due to its sovereignty disputes, it is a welcomed and positive player in the Indian Ocean.

Engaging with the island nations is a necessary shift to manage rising tensions and increasing geopolitical competition in the Indian Ocean. This and the previous chapters have captured the geostrategic importance of the ocean, and China's interest in and capacity for building its engagements with Indian Ocean nations. Chapter 3 in particular underlines the importance of SLOCs, how the different sub-regions together connect the wider ocean, and the ocean's importance to a rising maritime power. This chapter notes the role of island agency in shaping these geopolitical shifts in the Indian Ocean. The next chapter focuses on the role of island territories in the Indian Ocean. While it is assumed that infrastructure projects on island nations are hidden military projects undertaken by bigger players, there remains a geographic and strategic advantage for the traditional players of the Indian Ocean: their island territories. If Delhi, Paris, and Washington are seeking to manage competition in the Indian Ocean while addressing their respective strategic concerns, this aim could benefit from a two-pronged island approach. The first of these rests on engaging with the six island nations as sovereign nations, recognizing their agency as well as the issues that matter most to them. As noted in this chapter, island nations will come to play a key role in shaping great power competition, and their priorities and choices can no longer be pushed to the periphery of geopolitical conversations. Also, second, the traditional players of the Indian Ocean could and should leverage the maritime geography and strategic location of their island territories to secure, advance, and deepen their strategic and military priorities in the Indian Ocean. The next chapter takes this argument forward and in doing so it pays special attention to the islands of Andaman and Nicobar. Located in the eastern Indian Ocean, in close proximity to the Malacca Strait, these Indian islands hold unparalleled geographic advantages and offer a strategic solution to many evolving maritime security challenges. The next chapter, through the Andaman and Nicobar Islands, outlines both India's role in the Indian Ocean and the utility of island territories in managing Indo-Pacific military tensions. If Diego Garcia (Chapter 2) captures the strategic reality of the Indian Ocean in the post-1945 world, then the Andaman and Nicobar Islands highlight the future of Indian Ocean strategic dynamics.

5

Island Territories

Beyond an Unsinkable Aircraft Carrier

Chapter 5 provides an overview of the role island territories will come to play in shaping great power competition. As nations compete for power and access over key chokepoints and trading routes to bolster their presence and security across the Indian Ocean, island territories, much like island nations, will also come to play a significant role. These island territories, namely the Andaman and Nicobar Islands of India, Cocos Keeling of Australia, La Réunion of France, and Diego Garcia of the US/UK, along with the island nation of Mauritius, are key maritime assets which provide key traditional powers a geographic advantage in the Indian Ocean. In contrast to sovereign islands, in the island territories traditional players can choose to work toward their advantage in relation to the strategic landscape. These island territories played a secondary role during the colonial period and naval campaigns primarily due to their size and remote location. However, in the twenty-first century, the island territories might hold the military answer to traditional players' quest to maintain their influence and dominance while creating some deterrence for their competitors at key points across the Indian Ocean. To be able to do so, however, policymakers will have to shed the old perception of these island territories as "unsinkable aircraft carriers" and begin to think of their strategic value in terms of Maritime Domain Awareness (MDA), Intelligence, Surveillance and Reconnaissance (ISR), and anti-submarine warfare (ASW). If viewed in conjunction with island territories within the sovereignty of the Quad nations (India, Australia, the US, and Japan) and their partners, it provides an island chain that wraps around all entry and exit points to and from the Indo-Pacific. From Hawaii and Guam (US) to Tokyo and Okinawa (Japan), Cocos Keeling (Australia), Andaman and Nicobar Islands (India), Diego Garcia (US/UK and Mauritius), and La Réunion (France), these island territories provide access points to all the chokepoints identified in Chapter 3 as well as any movement across the Pacific, including the Indonesian straits of Sunda, Lombok, and Ombai Wetar. If these are viewed in combination with military facilities in coastal states, the Quad countries', along with France's, access to bases in Djibouti, Bahrain, Oman, Abu Dhabi, Bombay, Goa, Singapore, and South Korea only tightens the island chain that can ensure their military advantage through the Indo-Pacific.

This chapter argues for better utilization of island territories within the sovereignty of traditional players as well as for reducing competition over ports and roads in island nations for the purpose of great power competition. The idea is twofold—for the existing powers to develop their own territories for military purposes while collaborating with island nations to work on issues important to them—from IUU fishing and climate change to oil spills and disaster management. The geopolitical competition in the Indian Ocean will be defined by both traditional and non-traditional security issues at the same pace. However, there is a need to make the distinction between island nations and island territories and the approach toward each. In researching the island territories of the Indian Ocean, the Andaman and Nicobar Islands emerged as the most significant territory in shaping and influencing military presence in the Indian Ocean. Together with India's role in the Indian Ocean, this chapter provides an insight into India's maritime thinking and approach through the Andaman and Nicobar islands. In doing so, the author aims to capture the history of these islands as well as outlining the maritime thought of a nation often considered to be the net security provider in the Indian Ocean.

The Andaman and Nicobar Islands (ANI) are closely linked to the security of the Indian Ocean and India's maritime interests. Geography, more than anything else, has played a dominant role in deciding the fate of the islands and their indigenous population. Located near the Strait of Malacca, stretching across the Bay of Bengal, historically the islands have been an important way station linking the Indian Ocean and Southeast Asia. Despite their strategic location, however, the islands have remained on the fringes of maritime history. Although they have not so far played a central role in naval campaigns, the Andaman and Nicobar chain has captured the interest of navies aiming to establish dominance across the Indian Ocean. Similarly, the islands played a critical role in the British empire's broader strategy to control the Indian Ocean. It was one of the strategic island groups that helped in defining the ocean as the "British Lake."[1] The Japanese occupation of the islands in 1942 likewise had significant consequences for the power balance in the Indian Ocean, threatening British dominance in the region. However, Japan's withdrawal from the islands to address the emerging US threat in the Pacific pushed the islands back to British India. The subsequent events of World War II and the partition of the Indian subcontinent ultimately placed the islands within independent India.

This chapter aims to trace the importance of the ANI through India's maritime interests in the twenty-first century. It begins with a historical overview of the islands to understand their importance. Besides highlighting the role of the island chain, this section also examines the importance of islands in maritime thinking and naval warfare. Throughout history, islands have played a critical role in establishing dominance across vast theaters. As the great power competition continues to unfold in the twenty-first century, islands will again come to play a central role in maritime engagements. This chapter also briefly examines the role of islands during the Pacific War, the last major naval campaign of the past century. The US–Japan war began with an attack on the island of Hawaii and came to an end with the occupation of the island of Okinawa. The control of the Pacific islands between Hawaii and Okinawa played a decisive role in the war in favor of the victor. These lessons of the Pacific War are applicable today, as nations begin to readjust to maritime competition after decades of continental contests.

The second section of the chapter traces the conversation around the ANI in relation to independent India's strategic interests. Despite the strategic location of the islands, India's approach to them has been lackadaisical to say the least. This is not to say Delhi did not understand the importance of the islands, for the leaders of the freedom movement ensured the islands remained under Indian control during the partition of India and Pakistan. This section sheds light on the early conversations around the islands in independent India that shaped Delhi's approach toward the ANI. While Indian policymakers over the years have taken steps to grasp the importance of the islands, there was a lack of enthusiasm, and perhaps of a sense of urgency, to deliver on initiatives. The conversation around the ANI helps underline Delhi's overall approach toward maritime security in its strategic thinking, or the lack thereof. This section also underlines the challenges in realizing the potential of the islands, which are mainly related to their environmental constraints and concerns for the welfare of the indigenous people. That the challenges at times became an excuse for the lack of development on the islands speaks to India's maritime priorities.

The final section places the importance of the ANI in the context of a changing security environment characterized by increasing Sino-Indian competition. This section explores the opportunities and strategic potential offered by the islands as Delhi enters a new security environment within the Indo-Pacific architecture. Given the lack of development on the islands due to political neglect, this chapter examines options to leverage their geographic advantages. The maritime threats to India, and its naval priorities, are examined to provide a roadmap for the strategic use and development of the ANI. The importance of partnerships to help maximize the potential of the islands, and create a sustainable model for island development, is highlighted. As the Indian Ocean re-emerges as a theater for great power competition, islands today, including the ANI, will play a bigger role in deciding the power balance than they did as colonial outposts during World War II.

The Andaman and Nicobar Islands and their history

The Andaman and Nicobar Islands have found mention in many travelers' accounts documenting their journeys between the Indian Ocean and Southeast Asia. Indian scholars trace the earliest mention of the islands to the *Ramayana*, a Hindu mythological epic,[2] whereas most other accounts trace it more or less to the Greek astronomer Ptolemy, in the second century.[3] A more detailed narrative begins to emerge from the accounts of the Buddhist monk I-tsing and Venetian merchant Marco Polo, both of whom describe the islands and their people as barbaric. Marco Polo describes Necuveran (Nicobar) as an island where "they go all naked, both men and women, and do not use the slightest covering of any kind . . . there is nothing else worth relating."[4] On Andaman, the traveler describes its people with "heads like dogs, and teeth and eyes likewise . . . they are a most cruel generation, and eat everybody that they can catch, if not their own race."[5] I-tsing identifies the islands as the "country of the Naked People," where the natives "discharge some poisoned arrows" if travelers refuse to barter with them.[6] Similar narratives are found in many early accounts, including among Arab travelers, long before the official European advent to the islands. All such ancient and medieval accounts infamously recorded the people of the ANI as "wild beasts" who feed on "human flesh."[7] While the islands did not find much mention in Indian literature, they were consistently captured in a negative light, often being referred to as the home of *rakshasas* or demons.[8] Since then there have been many efforts to study the people, culture, language, and society of the Andaman and Nicobar group of islands, under both colonial rule and that of independent India. These studies show the early accounts of the islands carry grave misrepresentations of the people and their society.[9]

While travelers and merchants encountered these islands in their voyages between the Indian Ocean and Southeast Asia, naval commanders from different dynasties in the Indian subcontinent began to look to the ANI as a platform or a key strategic base to expand their reach and influence. One of the first accounts of the islands as an important naval base appears during the Chola dynasty of southern India. Rajendra Chola I undertook many naval expeditions (1014–1044), including against the Srivijaya kingdom (modern-day Sumatra, Indonesia), raiding port cities on the way.[10] The Andaman chain of islands proved strategic for all naval campaigns undertaken by Rajendra Chola I, establishing the islands as an important base for the Chola kingdom.[11] The desire to control the waters in the Bay of Bengal and secure communications with the trading nations of Southeast Asia led the Chola dynasty to raid, control, and use the ports in the Malay peninsula. Similarly, Kanhoji Anghre, the naval commander of the Maratha kingdom in the late seventeenth and early eighteenth centuries found the islands critical both in defense of its sovereign coast in western India and for naval expeditions.[12] Throughout the eighteenth century, European powers laid claims to the islands, underlining their importance for control of the trading routes between India and Southeast Asia. Although many empires—such as the Danish and the Portuguese—arrived on the islands, they were unable to establish or maintain a settlement due to the climate and disease on the islands, especially on the Nicobar Islands.[13] The British too occupied the islands in two phases, first in

1789 and again in 1858. The British abandoned the islands in the late eighteenth century due to disease and death before colonizing them again in 1858.[14] The arrival of the British, first through the East India Company in 1771, began a more formalized survey of the Andaman Islands and the surrounding waters.[15] These accounts documented the indigenous people of the islands in more positive light than those recorded in ancient and medieval times.

While there are varying descriptions of the indigenous people of the ANI, one fact is consistently reported across all documented accounts of the islands—their geographic and strategic importance. Aparna Vaidik, in her book *Imperial Andamans: Colonial Encounter and Island History*, captures the strategic importance of the islands in British Indian Ocean calculations, in detail. Vaidik disputes earlier historical accounts of the reason the British colonized the islands in 1858—that it was to establish a penal colony. According to archival documents, Vaidik asserts: "The colonization of the Andamans, as the contemporary colonial archives demonstrate, was part of the [East India] Company's larger political game to control the waters of the Indian Ocean stretching from the east African coast to Australia."[16] The penal colony was not the only reason for British interest, but a means to establish control over the islands, which were important for their strategic location. Another key assessment emerging from Vaidik's account is the repositioning of the islands in the world map. According to Vaidik, the islands were mapped as part of Southeast Asia and the Malay peninsula in early accounts, as they were critical in supporting travel to, and naval campaigns against, Southeast Asia. Colonial surveyors, however, placed them as strategic features in the Indian Ocean dominating key trading routes across the Bay of Bengal and the Strait of Malacca, linking their modern history to colonial India. The British essentially repositioned the "Andamans on the Imperial map, not as a segment of the Southeast Asian archipelago, but as a frontier outpost of the Empire in India."[17] Imperial Britain was the first European country to view the Andaman Islands as key to Indian Ocean security and not simply as a springboard to Southeast Asia. This difference, incidentally, carries far more significance in the geopolitical competition of the twenty-first century. The Andaman group of islands is now viewed as a strategic asset in controlling the entry and exit points to and from the Indian Ocean rather than a military outpost primarily supporting the Indian Navy's deployments to Southeast Asia.

Another important element that emerges through historical study of the strategic use of the islands is the notion that if the Andaman group of islands cannot be controlled (by the power seeking dominance across the Indian Ocean), it must be destroyed and kept out of enemy hands. This notion found strong support among the British and Japanese navies in the early twentieth century leading up to the Second World War. British officials in 1921 debated the role of the islands in the event of a war with Japan. While the islands at that point were not equipped to play a significant role in a war, British officials warned of the implications of abandoning the islands noting, "these islands . . . would be a serious menace, if they were occupied by a foreign hostile power."[18] The British in these instances were referring to a potential war with Japan in which the Imperial Japanese Navy might seek to occupy the islands to break British dominance over the Bay of Bengal and the eastern Indian Ocean. The Japanese, however, did not initially include the ANI in their original plan for the Burma Operation. The *Senshi Sosho* series[19] notes, "the Andaman Islands were also not mentioned at all in the Imperial Japanese Navy (IJN) Operations Policy decided on 5 November 1941 . . ."[20] The series, however, documents that the Imperial Japanese Navy later included the Andaman Islands in a list of "areas to be occupied or destroyed as swiftly as the operational situation permits" in their Indian Ocean operational map. That the Andamans were included along with islands such as Midway underlines that Japan recognized "the necessity of their capture or destruction at an early stage considering the strategic importance of the islands."[21] Japan's approach

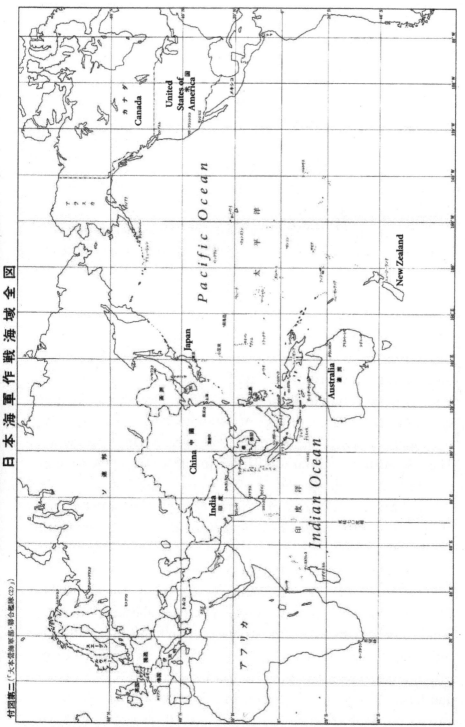

付図第二(「大本営海軍部・聯合艦隊〈2〉」)

日本海軍作戦海域全図

Canada

United
States of
America

Pacific Ocean

太　平　洋

New Zealand

Japan

China 中国

Australia 豪洲

Indian Ocean

印　度　洋

India 印度

アフリカ

Map 5. Imperial Japanese Navy's operational-strategic map, 1942.

toward the islands underlines the importance of geography in identifying islands positioned to offer strategic advantages or threaten the dominance of the ruling power. While the ANI may not have been central to any major campaigns, both Britain and Japan recognized the threat posed by the islands if they were occupied by adversaries or an enemy, which could threaten their dominance of and plans for (respectively) the Indian Ocean. Through the Andaman group of islands, the Japanese envisioned dominating the Indian Ocean and the subcontinent, pushing the Allies back from both.

Despite the significance of islands in maritime strategies, however, little attention has been paid to islands and their importance for maritime security today. That is beginning to change, however, as the conversation around a Taiwan Strait crisis is gaining momentum.[22] Most often, and especially due to the colonial history, islands have been recorded as way stations and logistics facilities in the recent past, relegating them to footnotes in the larger discussion on maritime strategy. In contrast, scholars have often used campaigns and battles around islands to illustrate strengths and weaknesses in maritime strategies. The US strategy of island hopping and leapfrogging is a popular narrative illustrating the role of islands in naval warfare. The US–Japan Pacific War was predominantly based on the strategic use of islands and geography.

War Plan Orange, the secret US strategy for the Pacific in the event of a war with Japan, relied heavily on geography to gain advantages in the theater. As Edward S. Miller notes in his book of the same name, "It is said 'that geography is the bones of strategy,' and so it was in the grand strategy of the Orange Plan."[23] According to Miller, "distance and geography dictated a three-phase contest" establishing American dominance across the Pacific.[24] Miller goes on to quote architects of the plan relying on Japan's greatest weakness: its dependence on seaborne commerce. Given the distance between the US Pacific Coast and Japan, Plan Orange relied on islands in the Pacific to establish bases securing their supply lines while using those very bases to cut off Japan's trading routes to "starve it of food, fuel, and raw materials." The need for bases became ever more important after the fall of Singapore in 1942 reduced Britain's ability to fight Japan at sea. The calculations for the cost and time required to establish a major base in the Pacific capable of supporting a naval campaign across the theater led to the decision to occupy a series of smaller existing islands' features. Miller notes, "The correct solution of the Phase II (the plan to develop a base supporting expeditionary forces to the Far East) . . . was to advance step-by-step across the Pacific by way of mobile bases set up on intermediate islands."[25] War Plan Orange relied on the understanding that, even if there were stronger land forces on the Japanese-occupied islands in the Pacific, whoever controlled the seas (by dominating the sea lines of communication—SLOCs) would have an advantage.[26] The key was to secure supply lines assuring reinforcements could be brought in. US aerial support in these islands proved critical in ensuring its own logistical support while denying it to the Japanese in the nearby islands. The strategy of island hopping eventually gave way to leapfrogging. Leapfrogging focused on occupying islands and bypassing enemy strongholds to establish superiority rather than spending time in occupying the islands one by one, including those with enemy bases. The strategy was to "bypass the strongest Japanese garrisons, seal them off by air and sea, and leave them to 'wither on the vine.'"[27] The US bypassed islands to reach Japan faster while the Japanese islands that were trapped between two US islands (via leapfrogging) lost their advantage.[28] Samuel E. Morison in his book, *The Two-Ocean War*, notes, "if we had continued in that pace [island hopping], it would have taken us years to reach Japan, and the enemy's strategy of tiring us out by sheer stubbornness might have worked."[29] The Pacific War underlines not only the importance of islands but also the role of geography in deciding the strategic value of islands. The Andaman and Nicobar Islands carry that strategic significance simply because of their geography. As noted, the ANI might not be the destination or the central element of a grand strategy, but its strategic geography means that it can influence the balance of power. This understanding of geography unfortunately is missing in independent India's strategic thought.

The British decision to establish a penal colony on the Andamans was based on its geography. The distance from the Indian coast to the islands was a good reason to send Indian nationalists and political prisoners to *kaalapaani*, or the black waters. The British hoped to weaken the freedom movement by creating a distance between the political prisoners on the island and leaders of the freedom movement on the Indian subcontinent. More than a hundred years after the establishment of the penal colony, the Indian political class used a similar logic of geography to protect Indian naval assets by sending them to the islands, given the physical distance and lack of communication between the Andamans and the Indian coast, during the 1971 Indo-Pakistani War. However, while independent India realized the geographic importance of the islands, it viewed them through a defensive lens, rather than seeing an opportunity. The islands were important not for the advantages they could give the Indian Navy but because it could be problematic "if they were occupied by a foreign hostile power."[30] This defensive outlook toward the islands framed the foundation for independent India's approach toward the islands. The focus remained on defending the islands from invasion with distant acknowledgment of their strategic potential, rendering the islands as a vulnerability or a liability rather than a geographic asset supporting India's maritime interests. Seventy-five years after independence, India has yet to utilize the islands to leverage the maritime advantages they offer, despite numerous studies and discussions highlighting this potential in the twenty-first century.

The ANI in India's maritime priorities

Independent India has been rather slow in realizing the potential of the ANI and this is primarily linked to India's outlook toward maritime security. India inherited a sizeable navy from the British, with geography favoring Delhi's position as a key Indian Ocean player. The lack of a maritime threat, especially after the end of the Cold War, combined with the absence of geopolitical competition in the Indian Ocean, helped Delhi emerge as a key Indian Ocean player. Instead of building on these advantages, however, Delhi grew complacent in its maritime role, pushing the Indian Navy to the bottom of its defense priorities. This was also a result of India's threat perception and the lack of strategic thought in leveraging its geographic advantages at sea. India's early military conflicts with China and Pakistan, in the 1960s, along the northern border, therefore shaped a lopsided continental defense outlook. While India is most certainly a maritime nation with a 7,500 km coastline,[31] its independent history does not support the notion of India as a maritime power. Although Delhi has taken significant steps to strengthen its maritime capabilities in the last two decades, its initiatives have been fairly basic. Tracing India's maritime developments through the 1960s and 1970s helps underline India's lack of a maritime vision and understanding of maritime geography in both its political and defense priorities. Delhi's approach toward the ANI in the twenty-first century is rooted in its political decisions during India's conflicts with China (1962) and Pakistan (1965 and 1971), which imagined the islands as a vulnerability.

The first significant development regarding the islands was in 1962, after the Sino-Indian War. Indian political leaders envisioned a possible threat from China toward the islands and tasked the Indian Navy with the garrisoning and defense of the ANI.[32] The navy had proposed establishing a physical presence on the islands in 1958, at a time when they had no defense structures or personnel. This request materialized, with the government sanctioning the stationing of the first Resident Naval Officer (RNO), who arrived at Port Blair in 1962 after the Sino-Indian War.[33] Subsequently, the first "Naval Garrison of five officers and one hundred and fifty six sailors arrived in Port Blair" in 1963.[34] However, it was the dismissal of the navy during the

Indo-Pakistani War in 1965 that perhaps laid the precedent for over-looking and undermining the role of the Indian Navy and the ANI. Admiral B.S. Soman's thoughts on the 1965 war,[35] as recorded in the official history of the Indian Navy,[36] are both astounding and telling with regard to India's lack of maritime thinking. Admiral Soman mentions that the primary responsibility of the navy after the 1962 war was the defense of the ANI. The priority of defending the islands did not come from an awareness of their strategic importance but from the fear of losing sovereign territory and the consequences of this for India's image in South Asia and the world. The need to defend an island chain geographically distant from the Indian coast placed the ANI as a vulnerability in India's military calculations, adding to India's responsibilities and requiring resources. This way of thinking, in subsequent years, actively discouraged Delhi from realizing the strategic potential of the islands. For India, any development on the islands first had to reckon with their vulnerability, which overshadowed their potential and the opportunities they offered. The lack of maritime understanding among Indian political leaders only strengthened this school of thought.

Delhi's approach toward defending the islands also sheds light on its limited maritime strategic thought. Noting the lack of cooperation from the other services and the priorities along the continental border, Admiral Soman recalls: "The army refused to even send a platoon there [ANI] and we had to raise our own land force with sailors in khaki uniform to man the various stations in these islands. So far as the navy was concerned, as soon as Pakistan started the trouble in Kachchh [1965], I had felt that my first priority would be these islands ..."[37] Admiral Soman also underlines a perceived threat from Indonesia toward the islands during the 1965 war. He notes:

I also had some intelligence on the presence of some Indonesian ships at Karachi and knew that any operation undertaken by the combined naval forces of Pakistan and Indonesia would neither be against the Indian Fleet nor the Indian mainland. It was most likely to be for the capture of the Andaman and Nicobar Islands. I was quite convinced in my mind that the Indonesian Navy, knowing full well that only a small force of sailors in khaki uniform was present on these islands, could make an attempt to capture the Nicobar Island despite the then pretty poor state of Indonesia's Navy.[38]

He goes on to elaborate on the restrictions imposed on the navy during the war, which he claims had a detrimental impact on how Delhi came to view the Indian Navy over the subsequent years. Admiral Soman had clear instructions from the Ministry of Defense saying, "The Navy is not to operate north of the latitude of Porbandar [on the western coast of India], and is also not to take or initiate offensive action at sea against Pakistan unless forced to do so by offensive action by the Pak forces."[39] Further, he met with then Defense Minister Y.B. Chavan to oppose such restrictions and limitations on the navy but was offered only caution and the argument that "it would perhaps be better if the navy did not go looking for trouble," acknowledging that the navy was continued to be overlooked after the 1962 "debacle."[40] Concerned about the "morale of the Service and the public perception of the Navy" sitting out during an active military conflict with Pakistan, Soman met with then Prime Minister Lal Bahadur Shastri to make a case for a naval engagement against Pakistan in an effort to minimize any threat against India and gain an advantage in the war. Shastri too stressed that the role of the navy in defense of the ANI was more important during the battle, reducing the navy's role to waiting for an attack from Pakistan and Indonesia. Soman pushed back, arguing "it was wrong in principle to tie down one arm of the Defence Services to passive action in a war situation,"[41] and that the navy was capable of both engaging in a military conflict and defending the ANI. Soman, as a last resort, requested to meet with the president as the supreme commander of the armed forces. The request was declined.

Delhi's approach toward the islands during the 1965 war brings out two perceptions. One, no arm of the Indian government either envisioned a maritime role or understood maritime engagement in an armed conflict. There appears to have been an unspoken rule among the political leaders that the navy was an inferior service. Unfortunately, the Indian political class neither invested in a maritime strategy nor understood the importance of its maritime geography in its armed conflicts. India, it appears, was unable to imagine engagement at sea as one of the responses to its continental troubles. This outlook continues to be a dominant thought to this day, as Delhi continues to view its land and maritime engagement in silos. Second, the 1965 maritime approach also strengthened the defensive outlook toward the ANI. Much of India's maritime development was undertaken from a defensive perspective through the 1960s. There were some developments, however, post the India–Pakistan war in 1965, aimed at improving the Indian Navy's capabilities. In fact, the decision to acquire Russian naval vessels in 1965 was linked to the defense of the islands.[42] The navy apparently found support in K. Subrahmanyam, who at that point was the deputy secretary for budget and planning in the Ministry of Defense, in acquiring Russian vessels and submarines. Subrahmanyam's reasoning was based on the lack of support from the US and UK in providing the necessary assets required by the navy, whose primary concern in 1965 was the defense of the ANI.[43] Despite such concerns regarding the defense of the islands, very little was done to improve capability and infrastructure on ANI itself.

In the lead-up to the 1971 Indo-Pakistani War, the navy had internal discussions on the role it could play in an armed conflict. The conversations, almost "bordering on an obsession,"[44] revolved around an aggressive role of the navy in the event of a war. The leaders in the navy called for strong role, noting, "we [the navy] must scrap, erase and wipe off from our minds any ideas of a defensive posture."[45] As India inched toward a war with Pakistan, the navy realized the role it could play in blocking all maritime communications between West and East Pakistan (now Bangladesh), trapping the Pakistani Navy in the Arabian Sea as Indian Armed Forces marched into East Pakistan.[46] As the naval headquarters started working on an operational plan for their role in 1971, there were questions regarding the *Vikrant*, India's then operational aircraft carrier. The initial suggestion was to leave the carrier in the Bombay harbor. However, Admiral S.M. Nand, India's then chief of navy, was against the idea. He recalls opposing the idea "because during the 1965 war also, VIKRANT was sitting in Bombay harbour and did not go out to sea. If in the 1971 war the same thing happens, Vikrant would be called a white elephant and Naval Aviation would be written off. Vikrant has to be seen as being operational, even if we do not fly the aircraft."[47] However, the decision regarding the *Vikrant* was challenging, bearing in mind the carrier could sink if attacked by Pakistani submarines, which would have irreversible effects on the image of the Indian Navy, and how it was perceived. The decision was further complicated by the fact that "VIKRANT's boiler had a crack and therefore the speed of the ship was restricted."[48] The navy's threat assessment estimated an attack on the *Vikrant* from PNS *Ghazi*, which led to the navy's decision to hide the carrier using the ANI, in its remote location, as a safe harbor. The navy's plan of action regarding the *Vikrant* was that it would be:

> secreted away at a remote anchorage, with no means of communication with the outside world ... Concurrently, deception messages started being originated to give everybody the impression that Vikrant was still operating between Madras and Visakhapatnam [in the Bay of Bengal].[49]

Vikrant was eventually deployed around the Bay of Bengal from the Andamans, but remained cautious, especially due to unfavorable wind conditions which hampered the launch of its aircraft.[50] Admiral Arun Prakash,[51] reflecting on the navy's role in the 1971 war, described the decision to deploy the *Vikrant* as a "gamble."[52] Regardless, the Indian Navy played a significant role in the 1971 war, especially in bombing the port of Karachi and destroying enemy forces and airfields and blocking supply lines in the Bay of Bengal, Cox's Bazaar, and Chittagong.[53]

While the navy's actions during the 1971 war are celebrated, it is considered inferior to the land and air forces. Despite the success of the naval operations in that war, including the geographic advantage provided by the ANI, the navy and the islands remained at the periphery of India's strategic and military priorities. This could have been for two reasons. One, Delhi made little effort to fully understand the strategic role of a navy and invest in maritime engagements. Second, the lack of an imminent threat at sea, along with limited resources, further pushed the navy to the bottom of India's defense priorities. Despite such limitations, however, the Indian Navy managed to gain an admirable position as an Indian Ocean power primarily supported by its geography and the lack of geopolitical competition through the late twentieth and early twenty-first centuries.

The next significant development regarding the islands was the creation of the Andaman and Nicobar Command (ANC), the only Indian Tri-Service Command, at Port Blair in 2001.[54] The ANC was a result[55] of the Kargil Review Committee, set up in 1999, after the Kargil War between India and Pakistan. The committee was tasked with reviewing the developments of the war and to recommend a course of action to avoid a similar situation in the future.[56] On the maritime front, the committee underlined the geographic distance of the islands from the Indian coast, highlighting their vulnerability to both traditional and non-traditional threats.[57] The establishment of the ANC was a significant step in placing all three services on the strategic islands. Given that the ANC is India's first and only theater-level command, it was expected to transform the role of the ANI.

Instead, the islands continue to be undermined with limited development and poor infrastructure for defense purposes.

The ANI, as a strategic but vulnerable asset, continues to dominate the political narrative in India's political discussions. The defensive view adopted in the 1965 war is the dominant approach in all conversation regarding the islands, even today. The islands could provide strategic advantages but their vulnerability, or rather the lack of a maritime strategy at the political level, has hindered realizing the potential of the islands. This narrative finds support even among leaders within the last decade.

As a former foreign secretary notes, "[At] some theoretical level we understand the importance [of the] ANI, but there is always something more important."[58] The official further attributes the lack of enthusiasm toward developing the islands to sea blindness and "leftover habits." Further, he explains, "Indian politicians see no point in raising maritime issues, there are no votes in that. People understand land, Pakistan."[59] He goes on to underline the lack of an "institutional focus in Delhi which has an interest in pushing this [strategic development of Andaman and Nicobar]." Moreover, the "MEA [Ministry of External Affairs] has limited bandwidth and attentive space." Sanat Kaul, who served as the chief secretary to the islands, described India's approach to the islands as "Masterly Inactivity" and "Benign Neglect."[60] A similar sentiment is echoed by a former senior official in the national security apparatus. Reinforcing the defensive approach to the islands, he notes, "[India] never looked at them [Andaman and Nicobar] as islands of opportunity, only as a territory to defend."[61] A defensive outlook toward the ANI also led to Delhi adopting a posture of limited development on the islands, to avoid drawing unnecessary attention to them. The reason for this was that rapid development and increased military infrastructure on the islands would create a sense of unease among India's neighbors, and especially China,[62] which might make matters worse for the islands given their preconceived vulnerability.

While Delhi, over the years, has taken steps to correct this inertia, the pace of development has been remarkably slow and further complicated by bureaucratic challenges. However, as the Sino-Indian competition continues to increase in the twenty-first century, the ANI are placed to play a critical role in leveraging India's maritime advantages despite their limited development. Political will, however, will be required to finally utilize the potential of the ANI.

The strategic value of island territories in the era of the Indo-Pacific

Development on the ANI has certainly come a long way since 1962, when the only significant defense structure was the airstrip in Car Nicobar (the northernmost of the Nicobar group of islands) built during the Japanese occupation of the islands in 1942. Developing the islands has also been challenging due to environmental concerns and concerns for the welfare of indigenous tribes on the island. The islands are considered a biodiversity hotspot, and the Indian government has strict measures in place to protect their ecological environment. As a result, 94.6% of the islands is under forest cover, making construction and development a challenging endeavor.[63] There are also indigenous tribes and communities across the islands who remain disconnected from the modern world. In an effort to protect the indigenous tribes, and rightly so, the government of India has passed many laws aimed at conserving these communities and their way of life.[64] While these concerns may have been genuine in the early days of India's independence, now the inability to find a creative way to address defense infrastructure while protecting the environmental and indigenous tribes stems from a lack of interest. The ANI are divided into two groups: the Andaman group (further divided into North Andaman, Middle Andaman, and South Andaman) and the Nicobar group (Car Nicobar, Little Nicobar, and Great Nicobar).[65] Together, the island chain numbers 572 islands, of which only 36 are inhabited.[66] India, therefore, has the option of building infrastructure and developing military facilities without interfering with the daily lives of the indigenous tribes. On the environmental concerns, as the founder of initiatives such as the International Solar Alliance[67] and Indo-Pacific Oceans initiative,[68] India has the opportunity to work with its strategic partners in creating a sustainable model for island development. India's partnership with nations such as France could provide the foundation for such an engagement, given Paris's experience with its overseas department of the island of La Réunion in the southwest Indian Ocean with similar environmental constraints and concerns.[69] Engagements in both La Réunion and ANI highlight the familiar environmental concerns as well as the military and strategic importance surrounding the two groups of islands. Paris in collaboration with island authorities have created a framework addressing La Réunion's unique biodiversity while maximizing the island's key strategic advantages. A concept of sister islands, pairing La Réunion and ANI, could provide Paris and New Delhi with a new policy roadmap for advancing its Indian Ocean collaboration.

In conversations with the strategic and retired naval community in Delhi on defense infrastructure over the years, any argument toward developing military capabilities on the ANI is immediately met with caution regarding the islands' vulnerabilities. These conversations also provide insights into India's concern about island defense. It appears that the opportunities offered by the islands will only outweigh the vulnerabilities if India fortifies its island defenses. Many senior retired Indian naval officers refer to Okinawa and Hawaii as ideal models for the role of islands in maritime security, suggesting there might lessons that can be borrowed for the ANI. Officials in Hawaii and Okinawa, however, rarely bring up island defense as a vulnerability and rather focus on the strategic advantages of islands as seen in World War II. For both the US and Japan have systems and mechanisms in place that cater to island defense as part of their national strategy.[70] It is not a separate or added conversation.[71] For

Okinawa and Hawaii, the advantage of geography dictates their role in national maritime strategies focused on SLOC protection through air and naval superiority. Borrowing from lessons from the Pacific War between the Imperial Japanese Navy and US Navy, a former commander-in-chief of the Maritime Self-Defense Force, Japan underlines the importance of air and naval superiority to establish and sustain SLOCs as the key elements of island defense. The vice admiral notes that the Imperial Japanese Navy "failed to defend an island because its SLOCs were cut off as a result of the loss of control of the sea and air. There is a direct relation between control of the air and sea and the success or failure of an island defense operation."[72] Furthermore, a serving senior US official in the Marine Corps Installations Pacific[73] in Okinawa, Japan, points to other challenges in island defense in the twenty-first century.[74] Responding to a question on US strategy for island defense in Okinawa, he notes, "The political risk of attacking an island like Okinawa, or for that matter any [island] with a civilian population, is incredibly high today. Increasing that risk could be a strategy in itself. If we are discussing a full-blown war, in the age of missiles, any island is equally targetable. It's about sustaining constant low form of competition and how we outcompete." He goes on to say "perceiving islands as 'unsinkable aircraft carriers' is a World War II narrative. We have gone beyond that and islands today provide elements of access and strategic advantage."

It is precisely this "access" that places the ANI at an advantage. The islands stretch close to the Strait of Malacca and the Indonesian Straits, which provides a significant opportunity for surveillance of movements into the Indian Ocean, especially of sub-surface vessels. Furthermore, this provides India and its maritime partners an added advantage in protecting and dominating key trading routes or SLOCs between the Indian Ocean and the Pacific. Building on this advantage will simultaneously address India's island defense concerns. The threat today, in the Indian Ocean, especially in the near future, is not so much that of a traditional military attack or invasion, but one that seeks strategic advantages against India. It is geography, and access to strategically located islands by a hostile power, that pose the most direct and immediate strategic and security threat. While there is no substitute for building the necessary defense capabilities on the ANI, it is short-sighted to overlook the advantages of island territories for fear of the possibility of an attack someday. In the current environment, and especially with China's growing interests in the Indian Ocean region,[75] the advantages and strategic choices offered by the ANI in shaping the new security dynamic outweigh possible vulnerabilities.

While political attention on the islands, particularly from a strategic point of view, has been inadequate, the Indian Navy has undertaken many studies and assessments to map a role for the ANI.[76] Similarly, the civil authorities in Port Blair too have their assessments of the implications of defense infrastructure for the islands. There is a disconnect between the defense establishment and the civilian authorities in Port Blair, where each at times views the other as a challenge to their priorities. The civil authorities are tasked with the overview of the welfare of the civilian population, including indigenous tribes, and is hesitant to share infrastructure and resources with their military counterparts. For example, the military requires an uninterrupted electricity supply to manage their equipment and surveillance platforms. Thus the civilian population at times suffers from electricity shortages so that military requirements can be met. The solution therefore lies in separate arrangements for critical infrastructure (electricity, water, etc.) for military and civilian purposes.[77] The military, for its part, is of the view that unless there is a vision and a strategy for the role of the islands in Delhi, the ANI will continue to suffer from ad hoc initiatives. Delhi must decide where the ANI lies in its national security and defense strategy, which would require institutional and structural changes in its governance to fully and sustainably realize the potential of the islands. Here again, La Réunion might provide a framework to work with Paris in realizing the delicate balance of biodiversity conservation and building military capabilities on the island chain.

In the last several years, however, India has made some attempt to upgrade the existing infrastructure on the islands, including airports and runways,[78] as well as aiming to transform the islands into a maritime hub.[79] The Narendra Modi-led government elected in 2014 (and re-elected in 2019) has also tasked different agencies to map and monitor developments of the islands,[80] and established the Island Development Agency (IDA) to lead holistic development of Indian islands to address its challenges.[81] While there has been increasing momentum in relation to the islands in the last five years, the pace of development has been slow and not aligned with India's changing maritime environment or interests. Another challenge with regard to the ANI is the perceived advantages they offer as India's "springboard" to Southeast Asia.[82]

There is a need to reimagine the role of the ANI. Over the last two decades, experts and officials alike have made an argument that the islands' significance lies in their proximity to Southeast Asia, and especially the Indonesian archipelago. While this is an important element, the advantage does not lie in the ANI as a military outpost supporting India's deployments into Southeast Asia, but as key hub for Maritime Domain Awareness (MDA), and for surveillance and intelligence missions keeping watch for threats coming into the Indian Ocean. Framing the ANI primarily around India's interests in Southeast Asia and its Look East policy undermines the potential and advantage of the islands. Southeast Asia and the South China Sea is a secondary area of interest for the Indian Navy.[83] Similarly, the Act East Policy[84] is an effort to strengthen India's political, diplomatic, and economic relations with ASEAN nations. India's naval role, capacity, and priorities in the waters around Southeast Asia are limited. Therefore viewing the primary advantage of the ANI as being a springboard to Southeast Asia overlooks its real potential, which is as strategic islands across a key chokepoint. It also reduces the urgency to develop and invest in the islands, pushing them down Delhi's list of priorities. Reframing the islands to support the role of the navy in issues around the Indian Ocean, the navy's primary theater, and as a hub for MDA, will help highlight their potential for Delhi.

India, in collaboration with its Indo-Pacific partners (the US, France, Japan, and Australia), can utilize its island territories and maximize its opportunities in the Indian Ocean.[85] For example, India and Australia can collaborate on MDA missions using their island territories of the ANI and Cocos (Keeling), by deploying their respective P-8 maritime patrol aircraft between the two islands.[86] Similarly, Delhi can maximize its maritime partnerships to access the islands of Réunion (France), Okinawa (Japan), Guam (US) and Diego Garcia (US/UK/Mauritius) to boost its MDA capabilities.

The Indian Navy has prioritized MDA and presence as a response to a new and changing security environment, and the rise of China.[87] The ANI are strategically located to address the navy's priorities. The recent Sino-Indian border conflict in June 2020 has increased tensions, widening the political mistrust between Delhi and Beijing.[88] There appears to be an agreement across the strategic community and policymakers on the need for a new China policy—one that would place Delhi in a position of power.[89] Although the confrontation is along its northern continental border, for the first time Delhi might be willing to explore its maritime advantages,[90] given Beijing's growing interests in the Indian Ocean and its Malacca dilemma.[91]

The ANI indeed provide a maritime advantage vis-à-vis China in the Indian Ocean. However, that advantage—for both the short and long term—must begin with MDA, including underwater surveillance.[92] As China increases its presence in the Indian Ocean, including through oceanography missions and deploying underwater drones,[93] "The need for a comprehensive Underwater Domain Awareness (UDA) strategy is pressing."[94] In order to strengthen its situational awareness of China's sub-surface vessels, India will find a strong need to monitor the straits of Sunda, Lombok, and Ombai Wetar along the Indonesian archipelago as the alternative routes to and from the Indian Ocean.[95] The ANI's location, close to the Indonesian archipelago, is ideal for monitoring, developing, and mapping threat assessments coming to and from the Indian Ocean.

The Sino-Indian competition today has extended from their continental borders to the maritime domain. While the Indian Navy holds a geographically advantageous position, it can be easily overcome if Beijing manages to establish and sustain a military base in the Indian Ocean. The current advantage lies in India's proximity to key trading routes through the ANI and partner island territories. India must look to leverage such opportunities and build on its advantages. Nations such as the US and Japan have advanced technology and knowledge of MDA and underwater surveillance.[96] As Delhi looks to strengthen its surveillance and UDA capabilities, its maritime partnerships with France, the US, Japan, and Australia— through island territories, intelligence sharing, and MDA missions— can provide the necessary support and resources to address a changing security environment. India should (albeit very belatedly) invest in and understand the strategic potential of the ANI in a new and emerging security environment.

As underlined in the beginning of this chapter, the ANI are strategically located, making them central to Indian Ocean security in the twenty-first century. The lack of a naval strategy, along with limited understanding of maritime geography, led to India marking the ANI as a vulnerability rather than an opportunity in its defense posture. Continued threats from the continental border, and the absence of threats at sea, widened the gap between India's land and air forces and its navy. Capital and resource constraints added to the challenges in realizing the potential of the islands.

This chapter argues in favor of reimagining the ANI in relation to Indian Ocean security rather than simply as a springboard for India's deployments to Southeast Asia in the current changing security environment. As Delhi adopts a more proactive approach to understanding the islands and improving their infrastructure, a clear vision for the ANI and their role in India's maritime security will help address the structural challenges. Finally, Delhi has an opportunity within its Indo-Pacific vision to leverage its partnerships in building and realizing the true strategic potential of the islands. As China continues to expand its presence across the Indian Ocean, strategic islands such as the ANI can offer significant advantages to India and its partners in a new geopolitical competition in the region, particularly in contrast to its troubles along the northern continental border.

6

Shaping the Next Decades of the Indian Ocean

The one thing no one is paying attention to, is how will India and China co-exist in the Indian Ocean.[1]

Maritime developments in the twenty-first century will reinforce the interlinkages between vast spaces, drawing out the need to view the maritime domain as a continuous space. The Hamas–Israel war that began on October 7, 2023 has had a significant maritime component. The Russia–Ukraine war, too, has had an impact on the maritime domain, from the Black Sea Grain Initiative to utilizing the maritime space for land-based strategic contests by disrupting shipping across the Red Sea. The attacks in the Red Sea by the Houthis from Yemen as a response to Israel's actions in Gaza from October 7, 2023, have significantly disrupted shipping in the Red Sea. They led to new coalitions and responses to protect shipping as well as to respond to the Houthis, a group of non-state actors. Although impacting the Red Sea most directly, these developments have security and economic consequences for a range of nations, from France to Australia and Japan. The point of using this example is to note that oceans are integrated in such a way that a development in one corner of the ocean will impact the larger theater. So, if a nation wants to secure its energy supply lines in the eastern Indian Ocean, it will also have to study and engage with developments in the western Indian Ocean to truly understand the challenges to its national security. To do that, there is a need to study the Indian Ocean as one continuous strategic theater.

The previous chapters argued for the need to view the Indian Ocean as one theater, and for the importance of the islands' views and agency; and they set out why the competition with China will be decisive in this ocean. It is worth noting once again that the book argues that the *competition* will be decisive in the Indian Ocean. With a better understanding of the region contextualized for the twenty-first century, what do the next decades look like? A unique feature of the Indian Ocean, through its many littorals, is that the ocean is truly the stage that underpins multipolarity. The sheer number of players, from big to small, with varying degrees of relevance—in terms of geography and economics, the military, and EEZs—could result in an infinite number of developments shaping the region in the future.

The geopolitics of the Indian Ocean region will largely be shaped through, first, the relationship between India and China across the Indian Ocean; second, the strategic use of fishing; and, third, the rising importance of climate-related security issues. This chapter also identifies the underwater domain as the next frontier for strategic competition and an arena which is clearly of significant national interest for both island nations and nations with maritime ambitions.

Asian powers at sea

The Sino-Indian competition will truly be a consequential competition for the Indian Ocean. Within the region, both are key players and partners for several littorals and island nations. While there is considerable history between the two Asian players on interactions along their continental borders along the Himalayas, including the 1965 Sino-Indian War, there is limited to no interaction at sea. India and China do not have any annual naval exercises, indicating a lack of direct communication or understanding of each other's views and approach to the maritime domain. The conflict along the land border, however, places heightened tension in the maritime domain. That India and China could go to sea and compete is not a new argument or observation, but this chapter aims to place the intensity of this competition against recent developments and their implications for the wider region.

As outlined in the previous chapter, India, from its strategic and defense perspective, can be categorized as a coastal nation but not a maritime nation. Maritime thinking within the political, strategic, and defense establishments in Delhi is limited and, for the most part, has failed to understand the advantages it holds. The lack of a wider maritime vision connected to its national security and strategy further contributed to the notion of the Indian Navy being the "Cinderella service."[2]

There is an argument to be made, to let the Indian Navy set the discourse on maritime partnerships and developments in the way the US INDOPACOM does. As India is a democracy, policymakers in New Delhi will always decide the trajectory of growth, expansion, and developments related to the navy; however, it is the navy that is perhaps the most strategically oriented of the armed forces in its long-term planning. If India has been able to establish itself as a key security player in the maritime domain, despite the navy's marginalized treatment within the armed services, then the credit for this rests largely with the navy. In assessing naval powers across the Indian Ocean, the Indian Navy truly emerges as a service that has delivered beyond expectations. A concerted effort to sustain and invest in its capabilities will be a key factor in balancing Delhi's competition with Beijing, both on land and sea. India's position in the Indian Ocean might ultimately present a deterrence to Beijing's aggressions in the sovereignty disputes on India's northeast and northwestern borders. The notion that upsetting China at sea might lead to negative consequences, or alter the status quo along its land border, is a reflection of both limited strategic understanding of the maritime domain and of India's own opportunities in the Indian Ocean. For long periods of time, India took cautious positions both in the maritime domain and in its partnerships to manage its relationship with China, including its approach to developing the Andaman and Nicobar Islands. However, as a nation with true great power ambitions, Beijing has followed—and will continue to follow—its roadmap to achieve this vision, which includes being present and securing its SLOCs in the Indian Ocean. What Delhi chooses to do, or refrain from doing, will have little effect on how China thinks and approaches the Indian Ocean, for security of the Indian Ocean is linked to Beijing's wider goals and ambitions, whereas managing the competition with India is perhaps limited to China's intentions in South Asia.

Recent military stand-offs and conflicts along the India–China continental border, and in particular during the Doklam incident in 2017[3] and deadly Galwan clashes in 2020,[4] however, significantly changed Delhi's view of Beijing. There is wider consensus within the political and military communities on China's strategic and military threat to India. For many, the India–China competition and conflict will perhaps be more damaging than the US–China competition, given the similarities between Delhi and Beijing, in terms of their geographies, their demographic and economic growth, and their relevance for each other as well as at the global level. While Beijing's narrative of Washington embarking on a strategy to contain China might attract some sympathy related to similar sentiments that long-standing global powers adopt a form of arrogant diplomacy, talking *to* the region (rather than *with*) and imposing their view of the world, the dynamics with India are significantly different, with the rise of both nations watched closely by most of the world. The Galwan incident underscores a viewpoint that China's rise to the global stage will include aggressive defense of its sovereignty, and, as it builds its military capability, this aggression will only increase. Therefore, what are India's options for managing and balancing the rise of its continental neighbor, which also has a strong partnership with Pakistan, Delhi's other neighbor, with whom it has also gone to war? The Indian Ocean might provide relief for the pressure points along India's continental borders, but will carry its own distinct implications for the region.

As Delhi is faced with direct challenges emerging from China's rise and ambitions, the Indo-Pacific presents itself as a theater of opportunity[5] to enhance Delhi's maritime capabilities through partnerships and geography. India's growing ties with its maritime partners, prominently with France, the US, Australia, and Japan, represent an opportunity to collectively address common maritime concerns as well as strengthen India's maritime capabilities. Today, the revival of the Quad in 2017, a grouping of India, Australia, the US, and Japan, is well placed to address individual threat perception and to offer collective maritime security to the region.

India's naval and maritime outreach in the last decade has been remarkable, and Delhi's acceptance of the strategic importance of the Indo-Pacific has played a key role in this. Despite considerable budget and resource constraints, Delhi and the Indian Navy have managed to re-establish India's role as a key player through positive investments and developments. If the Indian Navy's role in the 2004 Indian Ocean tsunami marked its place as a first responder, Delhi's vaccine diplomacy, carried forth by its navy, firmly established its dedication, seriousness, and ability to respond to and mitigate global crises. This new enthusiasm and outlook toward the maritime domain, however, accentuates the competition with China at sea. In the short term, India's role during a potential Taiwan Strait crisis will be hotly debated and watched by Beijing. The long-articulated Malacca dilemma will play out during any potential Taiwan Strait military crisis. However, it is unlikely that any nation, including the US or India, will actively disrupt Chinese energy lines across the Indian Ocean during such as crisis, as that would significantly escalate the risk of wider military conflict. There are also serious concerns over both the capacity for, and capability of, identifying Chinese vessels and disrupting their movements, given the high volume of traffic that transits these waters every day. At the same time, no action being taken around these chokepoints during any potential Taiwan Strait crisis will help Beijing test out its Malacca dilemma, and perhaps gain further confidence in mitigating its geographic disadvantages in the maritime domain around these straits. This will be a contingency that Beijing will be looking to address, while the US and its partners will look to disrupt these efforts. Given the location of the Andaman chain of islands and the Indian Navy's capabilities around those waters, Delhi's role in such a situation will be crucial. While the level of engagement from India can be debated, there is little room for Delhi to remain on the sidelines altogether. This would also be the right time to establish foundations of deterrence from India in the Indian Ocean, to slow China's advancing presence in the Indian Ocean. As noted in Chapter 3, a second Chinese Indian Ocean military facility is imminent. Once that development occurs, the Malacca dilemma only weakens, as Beijing will have stronger options both in the western Pacific and the Indian Ocean. Regardless, a limited conflict in the western Pacific will also have an impact on the Indian Ocean, and will either accelerate the Sino-Indian competition at sea or create further mistrust between the two Asian capitals. Either way, India and China's interaction and presence in the Indian Ocean will be a key factor both for the wider Sino-US competition and the security environment in the Indian Ocean.

Weaponizing fishing

Illegal unregulated and unidentified fishing will command a critical role in defining the security issues of the Indian Ocean in the coming decades. While on the surface it is a conversation about the impact of illegal fishing on the economy and livelihoods, it has wide-ranging implications, from geopolitics to leveraging technology for strategic purposes.

The Cod Wars in late 1950s and early 1960s between the UK and Iceland are a reminder of military conflicts over "non-traditional" security issues.[6] The lines between traditional and non-traditional security issues will continue to blur in the coming decades across the Indian Ocean. Although much planning and conversation goes into preparing for potential contingency over limited military conflict around the Taiwan Strait, there is equal potential for conflict at sea emerging from issues considered non-traditional security such as IUU fishing. A version of the Cod Wars in the twenty-first century will be much more consequential with the advance in technology and its applications to naval and maritime strategies. During peace-time, fishing rights, as noted by officials in Madagascar in Chapter 4, can fuel geopolitical competition. The dual use of "soft security" developments and issues, empowered by advanced technology, will intensify geopolitical competition at sea. For instance, fishing vessels can and at times have already become a marker for "presence" and interests. Economic interests will also draw military protection. A crucial challenge for China in the Indian Ocean is its operational inexperience in the theater. As the People's Liberation Army (PLA) Navy is not based here, it needs significant experience and opera-tional capabilities in the Indian Ocean. This begins at the funda-mental level of understanding the domain, mapping the Indian Ocean, and studying its currents, depths, and patterns. Today, many of these intentions can be realized by fishing vessels equipped with high-tech sensors, radars, weapons, and the ability to stay at sea for longer periods of time. Developing its submarine deployment routes requires a better understanding of the bathometry of the oceans, in particular the depth, warmth, and salinity of the waters. These metrics can today can also be mapped and picked up by fishing vessels, along with scientific and research vessels. Conversations about fishing are no longer about mitigating IUU fishing, although that remains front and center in identifying maritime security issues in the Indian Ocean.

Another example of a non-traditional threat and the use of dual technology is MDA. As outlined in Chapter 4, small island nations are actively looking for partnerships to advance their MDA capabilities to secure their EEZs from maritime crimes such as IUU fishing, smuggling, and trafficking. The need for MDA is so urgent and so strongly related to national and economic growth that it has become an essential requirement for coast guards and navies. However, the assets, equipment, and technology to conduct MDA missions and create a viable picture to monitor movements at sea lies with bigger powers. As islands continue to seek their path in developing their own MDA capabilities, bigger powers' ability to offer surveillance, patrols, and presence in key waters in across island nations to address non-traditional security threats further aggravates geopolitical competition. The dual use of maritime security for military advantage is not new. In the Indian Ocean itself, the first time the PLA Navy deployed its submarines to the region was in support of its anti-piracy missions in the Gulf of Africa. The use of submarines, which is incompatible with addressing a "non-traditional security" threat such as piracy, is a useful reminder of dual-purpose strategic initiatives which contribute to competition. While submarines may not have been a necessary asset for Beijing's anti-piracy missions, the Chinese presence in the area—which was centered around providing a global common goal—allowed for two consequential developments: the deployment of its first submarines to the Indian Ocean and the establishment of Beijing's first ever military facility in Djibouti.

As with continental silos, there is a need to stop dividing security issues into traditional and non-traditional categories. Island nations are perhaps correct in urging bigger powers to take on a more comprehensive approach to security, where economic and development needs can lead to military and national security threats. The definition of what constitutes "security" will continue to shift, and competing powers will be forced to coordinate and examine their respective approaches to non-traditional and traditional security issues in order to create their own assessments of threat perception.[7]

Climate change and the blue economy

Climate change already has become a key security concern for the region's militaries today, and its impact on preparedness and posture is being assessed.[8] However, for many island nations and littoral states, the need for action and change is immediate as climate change is posing national security risks. While bigger nations are now beginning to consider and accept the implications of climate change on security, islands have been at the forefront of this conversation for the last three decades. In their view, the current pace of action does not match the urgency at hand, with many nations calling for bigger and better responses to the climate crisis.

Climate change poses the risk of accelerating all maritime crimes, especially those identified by island nations in Chapter 4. Issues such as migration, smuggling, displacement, and drugs will increase and create existential crises for island nations at sea. As islands face the immediate impacts of climate change, their vulnerability to the crisis and the urgent need to protect their EEZs might see competition over development projects, aid, and assistance accelerate. Heightened tensions over dual use of development projects will exacerbate geopolitical competition, placing island nations in a challenging position of balancing great power interests while addressing national security threats emanating from the climate crisis.

The climate crisis will also challenge existing frameworks, agreements, and treaties. Vanuatu's decision to ask the ICJ for an advisory opinion on climate change sits outside of the Court's traditional realm of cases. However, the UN General Assembly's support for Vanuatu's choice of asking the ICJ for an opinion underlines growing support for small island nations' fight against climate change. This will, in turn, bring into question the relevance, applicability, and significance of a world order debated and constructed at the end of World War II, and its ability to address the challenges of the twenty-first century. At the UN, if bigger powers will look to smaller nations for diplomatic support on issues important to them, small island nations, too, will closely monitor the nations standing by them through votes and co-sponsorship of resolutions important to them. The climate crisis will most likely create further division between the global north and global south. Combined with the political baggage of nuclear tests and colonialism, the climate crisis will likely add to growing discontent toward western powers that contributed significantly to the climate crisis for their own development without heeding the consequences. In turn, island nations and littoral states will find themselves in the crosshairs again, paying for the actions of bigger powers while also becoming the theater for their competition for power. The challenges of climate crisis stand to create such urgencies with regard to national security that nations might move away from traditional partners to players with knowledge of, and interest in, mitigating the climate crisis, rather than providing military security. India and China will perhaps play a unique role in the climate conversations in that they would be both contributors to the crisis and allies in addressing it.

Addressing climate change through mitigation, adaptation, loss, and damage will become an important tool for foreign policy engagements and in forging strategic partnerships. While partnerships between nations will be based on mutual national security interests, in the twenty-first century, "non-traditional" issues will play as much of a role as traditional security issues. Climate science, such as studying the impact of climate change on fish movements and patterns, will have implications for economic security. Issues that stem from climate change are interconnected and will come together to define national and economic security concerns for many nations, big and small, albeit at different scopes and levels.

A division of traditional and non-traditional security issues, as well as the habit of viewing maritime spaces in silos, have led to a fragmented understanding of the Indian Ocean. India could have perceived a stronger China in the Indian Ocean when Chinese submarines docked in Sri Lanka in 2014, en route to assist in the piracy mission in Gulf of Africa. While Delhi noticed its maritime neighbor accommodating Beijing's submarines calling at Sri Lanka's port, it failed to connect this to the vessels' destination in Africa and the wider implications of China's interests and ambitions across the Indian Ocean. India perhaps also dismissed China's ability to present any sort of a strategic threat in the Indian Ocean, given its conceived notion of being a favorable partner to island nations across the Indian Ocean. Much like Washington in the western Pacific today, Delhi too was measuring red lines through the prism of a worst-case scenario, which is to say, can China go to war with India in the Indian Ocean and win? The answer remains no, but can Beijing undertake a series of initiatives and engagements which could complicate India's threshold for a red line? The answer is yes. There is a lot that can happen between increasing interests, and presence, and limited conflict. It will all play out during the stage of strategic competition, for which the Indian Ocean will be the central theater.

The blue economy as a strategic tool

While there are many definitions of the blue economy—states and international organizations define it in line with their priorities, capacities, and regions of interest—the core understanding remains the same. It is about a sustainable way of tapping into the ocean to generate an economy without compromising the marine ecosystem. The common sectors of the blue economy are fishing, tourism, and port-related activities. These sectors generate employment and allow states to create a market offering services and products within these sectors. Simultaneously, initiatives focused on clean water, renewable energy, biodiversity protaction, and pollution-free oceans focus on maintaining a healthy ocean without depleting its resources. The security threats to the blue economy include illegal fishing, natural calamities, and the use of the ocean for illegal activities such as smuggling and terrorism. These sectors—resource extraction, sustainable methods, and secure seas—together offer a conducive climate for an effective blue economy.

A focus on maritime security has brought the potential and resources of the ocean to the fore. While island states have engaged with these issues for a long time, global attention to such aspects has had a significant effect, making them a critical component of maritime security. However, conversations about ocean resources have to be accompanied by the sustainable use of the ocean while protecting marine life and keeping the oceans clean and safe.[9]

There is no doubt that the blue economy is a productive and necessary initiative to address maritime concerns and an opportunity to advance island economies. However, it requires significant capacity, including military, capital, research, and other resources to achieve this goal. For instance, in order for a nation to sustainably use its oceans for different sectors of blue economy, it must ensure that its coastal waters are secure for its own use and purposes. It must also ensure that the marine resources in its coastal waters are protected for the nation's use, and resources are not lost through illegal fishing and other activities. This can be achieved through maritime patrols and surveillance undertaken by the national navy and coast guard. Given the large EEZs island states generate, the ability to protect and monitor their waters is also directly related to protecting their sovereignty. If an island state cannot protect its large EEZ due to a lack of resources and capabilities, it might ask for assistance from a larger maritime partner to secure its coastal waters—which, in return, will increase the influence and stakes of the nation providing net security.

The possible use of benign non-traditional collaborations carrying deep strategic significance in the twenty-first century is perhaps best highlighted by China's Belt and Road Initiative (BRI). Responding to a regional demand for better infrastructure, in 2013 China launched the Maritime Silk Road (later renamed the Belt and Road Initiative) to boost connectivity and infrastructure between China, Europe, and Africa, running across continental Asia and Europe, and the Pacific and the Indian oceans. The primary focus of Beijing's initiative has been on island states and littorals, with an emphasis on infrastructure development through building ports, airports, highways, and roads, among others.[10]

Given the strategic locations of the recipient nations, there has been a growing debate on the advantages such commercial initiatives provide to China strategically and militarily. Over time, countries such as India, Japan, and the US have been vocal in questioning Beijing's intentions regarding its connectivity projects. In 2016, India's then foreign secretary, S. Jaishankar, noted that countries can use connectivity "as an exercise in hard-wiring that influences choices."[11]

China's increasing presence and engagements with the littorals of the Indian Ocean region, through both commercial and strategic engagements, is of growing concern to countries such as India. Combined with Beijing's approach toward international rules and norms in the maritime domain, highlighted by its behavior in the South China Sea, it is of concern for other security actors as well, such as France, the US, Japan, and Australia.

As the debate around a new regional security architecture gains traction, scholars and analysts have highlighted the importance of islands in this new geopolitical competition.[12] Given the importance of addressing non-traditional threats to island nations, collaborative initiatives such as the blue economy also carry a strategic dimension. Although blue economy initiatives are focused on cooperative development, one cannot separate out the underlying strategic imperatives of such collaborations. For instance, investments made by competing powers in the blue economy can be understood as aimed at gaining strategic leverage. China's Belt and Road Initiative and investments in the Indian Ocean region are perceived with growing concern by Delhi as a means to gain strategic leverage in the Indian Ocean.[13]

Growing Sino-Indian competition in the Indian Ocean region will only highlight such differences. Investments may vary from building commercial ports to high-end resorts, increasing the stakes of the investor in the region. For instance, an increased collaboration between the islands of Madagascar and Comoros with China for surveillance of their coastal waters will allow for an increased Chinese presence in the Indian Ocean. Even if the assistance provided is for a productive collaboration such as the blue economy, one cannot over-look the strategic advantage such collaborations would offer a new rising power in the Indo-Pacific. The ability to maintain a presence through collaborations in Madagascar and Comoros would mean that Beijing could gain operational experience and an opportunity to maintain a presence in the western Indian Ocean, close to key choke-points and trading routes such as the Mozambique Channel, Bab-el-Mandeb, and the Strait of Hormuz. The increased need for surveillance and monitoring of coastal waters, and the underlying strategic signif-icance of this, has placed the Small Island Developing States (SIDS) at the center of geopolitical competition. Many of these islands have vast EEZs with little capacity to monitor and secure their coastal waters. Most often, these states turn to bigger neighbors or partners for security, which includes surveillance of EEZs to mitigate illegal fishing and monitor illicit activities, such as drug smuggling and human trafficking. Maritime piracy is one of the oldest non-traditional security threats in the domain. That surveillance and monitoring has a direct connection with traditional security issues requires no new emphasis. For instance, the first time China deployed a nuclear submarine in the Indian Ocean was for its anti-piracy mission, a non-traditional security concern.[14]

With growing competition over, access to, and leverage over these crucial waters, islands are becoming a new theater for competition among big and middle powers. As this geopolitical competition extends to the non-traditional sector, the blue economy will emerge as a key area of interest for maritime collaborations. Although there is a recognition of the importance of the blue economy, there is little research and study to identify a development model. There is a serious need for research and development on the blue economy to attract capital and investments to help realize the potential of the oceans. While the investments will come from international organizations or big regional actors, the initiatives are being led by small coastal states that are directly affected by climate change and are looking for new ways to tap into the ocean to boost their economy.

As the island states turn to new actors, such as China, in seeking assistance and funding to address their capacity constraints, there is a high risk of increasing strategic mistrust and competition among the key players in the Indian Ocean region. Suspicion and concerns might hamper progress and change the security environment of the region. The island states must also be conscious of this possibility when leasing and providing fishing rights and other licenses to carry out scientific studies and deep-sea mining; such activities have very serious implications for traditional maritime security challenges.

The blue economy in the Indian Ocean region has great potential and the island nations of the western Indian Ocean, especially Mauritius and Seychelles, are playing a critical role in highlighting its importance to the region. However, there is a need for countries with converging interests to come together and offer alternatives, projects, assistance, and funding in order to mitigate the risk of one player dominating the strategic landscape in the Indian Ocean.

In an effort to develop its blue economy, Mauritius has identified fishing and aquaculture, tourism, and port-related activities as the priority sectors. Sustainable fishing is one of the key sectors of the blue economy given the expansive marine resource in the oceans.[15] For Mauritius, it is a significant market given the fish stock in the Indian Ocean, especially stocks of tuna, for which there is remarkable demand in European and Asian countries. With an EEZ of 2.3 million square kilometers, the fishing, aquaculture, and seafood processing sector of Mauritius' ocean economy accounts for 9.1% of export earnings. In its aim to maximize returns from the ocean economy, the government is keen to foster the "emerging sectors" (aquaculture, maritime services, and marine commerce) and the "nascent sectors" (marine biotechnology, offshore oil and gas, and marine renewable energy).[16]

In terms of types of fishing, Mauritius focuses on tuna fishing and its waters are primarily surrounded by European (French, Spanish) and Asian (Korean, Japanese, and Chinese) vessels. The government also offers fishing rights for industrial fishing in an effort to boost investments. These activities are monitored by the Mauritius government as well as the Indian Ocean Tuna Commission (IOTC).

In line with its ocean economy efforts, Mauritius is now looking to develop a new strategy focusing on sustainable stocks, while diversifying markets and end products. Such an effort begins with the need for surveillance and a survey of stock assessments. It requires EEZ protection to mitigate illegal fishing. The Mauritius government is keen to develop capacity for constant monitoring of stocks to enable sustainable fishing. There is also keen interest in studying the changes in the ocean—the rise in water level, wave patterns, and changes in the marine environment—to better prepare the fishing industry and support its activities, to be aware of pollution, and to detect early signs of any possible natural disasters. Mauritius has collaborated in acquiring German technology to enable its surveillance capacities. Officials in the government also mentioned the need to assess applications of Big Data to determine stocks. While surveillance and monitoring of the EEZs are important, there is also a strategic and political aspect to such collaborations. Assets, experience (technical, scientific), and capital are required. Due to an increasing interest in the western Indian Ocean by new and rising actors, assistance in surveillance and monitoring may result in gaining critical data that might address strategic concerns. It is extremely important that such data is handled carefully and shared responsibly with actors and players without compromising the security environment of the region. Surveillance is also critical to determine whether illegal vessels are operating in the region. Lack of proper vessel registration and spoofing are some of the challenges that remain.

Beyond the development of traditional sectors in the blue economy, Mauritius is engaged in boosting two other areas heavily reliant on technology. Mauritius is perhaps one of the first small island countries to have acknowledged the potential of technological applications in the maritime domain. One such application is the development of the Deep Ocean Water Application (DOWA) program. The program uses the natural properties of the ocean to cool commercial buildings, using cold sea water instead of electricity to provide air conditioning for office space. The government has welcomed private sector collaboration in developing the project and it is a continuing effort. The program pumps water from a depth of 1,000 m at −5°C which is transferred to an energy station. The Mauritius Economic Development Board description says: "the Deep Ocean Water Application (DOWA) leverages the natural characteristics of nutrient rich, cold deep-ocean water for the development of high value-added commercial activities supported by new technologies and industrial know-how. These activities range from Sea Water Air Conditioning (SWAC), Green Data Centers, high-end aquaculture, pharmaceuticals, and thalassotherapy, among others."[17] An ongoing project aims to provide green cooling to public and private buildings at the center of Port Louis. Another project is reviewing the commercialization of Ocean Thermal Energy Conversion. According to the Mauritius Economic Development Board, "The exploitation of deep sea water in Mauritius will foster the emergence of a new industry."[18]

The other sector Mauritius has the potential to tap into, and is keen to leverage, is to offer the island as a data hosting and data transfer hub. An interesting development in this sector is the emergence of underwater data centers. Big technology companies have huge data centers that require constant cooling, using significant space and energy resources. The underwater data center concept uses the ocean as a storage space, facilitating bringing the data centers close to a direct cooling and energy source and thus mitigating the need for real estate and high energy consumption. Companies such as Google and Microsoft are considering such underwater centers and Microsoft has in fact initiated a program which is in the trial phase. Releasing a statement on the program, the company stated, "Microsoft is leveraging technology from submarines and working with pioneers in marine energy."[19]

Mauritius's ambitions to harness the new and innovative potentials of the blue economy might make it a hub for the IT sector. If realized, underwater as well as offshore data centers will boost both the investments and presence of the technological and digital giants on the island, and will contribute to making Mauritius an IT services hub. However, again, such research and studies might affect strategic interests and must be approached with care. If underwater data centers study submarine functionality, they might also produce new data about submarine deployment for interested rising powers.

Regardless, Mauritius's approach to utilizing the economic benefits of the ocean shows the impact island nations will continue to have in shaping the geopolitical and economic debate in the maritime domain. It also advances the application of emerging technology in the maritime domain, a key nexus of emerging technologies, geopolitics, and economics in the oceans, and particularly in the deep sea—the least-studied domain in human history.

The next frontier: The commercialization of the deep sea

Discussions, policies, and governance regarding underwater domain resources are limited. Mostly they operate under two streams—military applications and oceanography— and for very specific purposes, with a focus on anti-submarine warfare and marine science. Unlike at the surface level, the policy debate is yet to understand, research, and write on the advent of or the implications of the underwater domain in geopolitics.

Mapping the underwater domain will emerge as a central tenet of geopolitical competition ranging across military, scientific, techno-logical, and governance aspects. In the coming decades, the geopo-litical competition across the maritime domain will begin to play out across the ocean floor and at different ocean depths. In my view, there is a convergence between fishing, marine research, and surveying. Hydrography, ocean policy, and deep-sea mining: the silos within each of these pillars of the oceans are beginning to overlap for geopolitical and strategic advantage. For instance, to be able to deploy submarines, it is important to study the ocean floor and the physical, biological, and chemical features of the ocean. The science and data which provide insights into marine life deep in the ocean also provide insights into deploying, detecting, and hiding military submarines in the oceans. As technological advances develop dual purposes, studies undertaken for commercial or ecological understanding of the oceans can also aid a nation's interests in submarine and anti-subma-rine warfare. For a new player such as the PLA Navy, the decision to enter any military conflict in the Indian Ocean will be based on years of oceanographic research, which is already well underway. This is also Beijing's biggest and most vulnerable domain in the Indian Ocean. The more Beijing attempts to understand the ocean floor across the region, the more it will impact increasing geopolitical competition. Moreover, now there is an increasingly blurred line between oceanographic research and strategic and military interests, making scientific research and presence across oceans a concerning development.

Combine that with the private sector now potentially accessing the deep sea—say for obtaining critical minerals through seabed mining. Fishing activities undertaken by private companies for economic purposes also saw the emergence of a range of illegal crimes and activities at sea. This has had an impact on naval capacities and responsibilities to keep the oceans safe and secure. IUU fishing is a major security concern in the Indian Ocean today. Going forward, when—and it is a matter of when and not if—the private sector has access to the deep sea for commercial purposes in international waters, navies will need to prepare to respond to any developments, including traditional and non-traditional security risks emerging from such economic activities. Given there are no frameworks, legal treaties, or governance models on commercializing the deep sea in international waters, we might be faced with a challenge where technological advances will push maritime security to a place without established norms and rules. This is not an argument against the use of emerging technology in the maritime domain, rather an argument to discuss, debate, and understand the importance and need for treaties and agreements on accessing, extracting, and commercializing the resources found in the deep sea. There are not nearly enough debates and studies into understanding and researching the impact on maritime security of opening up the commercialization of the deep sea. This in turn will have an impact on geopolitical competition.

The ability to operate on, over, and under the water is an important pillar for nations with naval and maritime ambitions. The ability to sustain vessels and flags across seas and oceans will be an important marker to establish maritime interests and capacities in the Indian Ocean. Today, this goal can be achieved by both the traditional and non-traditional maritime presence of the military as well as non-military or commercial vessels. An increased commercial presence across the maritime domain in areas such as sub-sea telecommunications cables, deep-sea mining, and toward the support of the blue economy will simultaneously increase the need for military presence and capabilities. The flag always follows trade. Now, this competition will be played out in one of the toughest domains: the underwater. In terms of military research, a primary goal for an emerging player like China will be to better understand the very challenging underwater domain of the Indian Ocean. From a strategic viewpoint, exercises undertaken to build capabilities, knowledge, and capacities in areas such as undersea cables and deep-sea mining can also aid efforts in mapping the underwater domain in the Indian Ocean, supporting a navy's quest to better understand this domain for military operations. The point being, there is an increasingly blurred line between non-traditional and traditional security threats. Developments concerning undersea cables and deep-sea mining—areas that are studied under technology and energy security—tomorrow will carry significant implications for militaries operating on, over, and under the seas.

In the coming decades, geopolitical competition in the underwater domain will dramatically increase, and will see the intersection of science and technology, the private sector, governance, climate change, and military security. Much more debating and thinking is needed regarding the intersection of these areas and the implications for maritime security and geopolitics. These developments will continue within their silos regardless. The question is: are policymakers prepared to respond, govern, and protect the seas and oceans from the challenges of the twenty-first century?

Conclusion

Maritime security as a foreign policy tool

The maritime domain today has a distinct relevance to foreign policy priorities. Foreign ministries, navies, climate scientists, and ocean policy all have equal and growing interest in the domain. Together, these interests have pushed the relevance of the maritime domain up the list of priorities in foreign policy calculations.

The world is in a new era of competition. While competition in itself is not a new phenomenon in a changing security structure, the nature, framework, and the players themselves are significant in this competition as it unfolds through the twenty-first century. Geopolitical competition has always been studied through the lens of great powers. That needs to change today to truly understand the complexity of the competition we find ourselves in globally. Far more players have greater stakes, interests, and, most importantly, capabilities and capacities to impact and influence great power competition than ever before in history. This is perhaps the beginning of an era where small nations, with a fraction of power in terms of size, military strength, and population, can impact power rivalries within their neighborhoods. Failure to recognize and manage this agency of small powers will have an exhausting impact on resources for bigger nations.

For instance, the choices and foreign policy priorities of, say, the Maldives will have a significant impact on India's security environment. Malé's right and choice to expand its partnerships with nations beyond its traditional ones could and may trap India in a revolving door of deploying resources to mitigate short-term challenges and being pushed to the sidelines for being a dominant neighbor. This in turn will reduce India's ability to use its resources and capacities in other areas of interests and for other priorities. Similarly, in the Pacific, Papua New Guinea's foreign policy choices could have a great security impact on Australia's interests. If we have studied the Maldives in the context of India's strategic environment, we will now also have to study the Maldives' foreign policy priorities to understand India's security environment. There is a need to shift the policy lens and rearrange our perspectives so as to understand the great power competition ahead of us. This, in turn, requires the study of the maritime domain as a geopolitical tool and a critical domain for national security and foreign policy interests. Discussions of the Indian Ocean and its role in the Indo-Pacific are long overdue. Like the Indian Ocean, maritime security has too often been studied in silos, divided into naval and military matters, ocean policy, climate, trade, and economics. Each of these aspects is then viewed in the context of continental priorities, diminishing their maritime relevance.

Maritime security today is an active tool for foreign policy engagements. A domain which was largely shaped, debated, and discussed by the naval and the sea-going community has emerged as a critical tool for policymakers and politicians. However, a key difference is that while the military or the navy studies the oceans as one continuous component or theater, policymakers, for generations, have not undertaken the effort to study and understand maritime security. Without this wider understanding of the maritime domain, policies crafted for engagements in maritime security by those who formulate foreign policy will tend to fall short of meeting its requirements. Understanding this domain, its challenges, its shape, flow, and implications will therefore become an important aspect of studying foreign policy and strategic security. It is time we began to study the oceans and the maritime domain as a foreign policy toolkit, rather than separating it into silos of commercial shipping, military strategy, and climate change. Each of these is interconnected, and together they strongly shape the foreign policy of each particular nation.

The wider argument for studying the maritime domain so as to understand geopolitical competition is in order to step away from continentalization of the maritime domain. If policymakers continue to study the Indian Ocean through the lens of South Asia, Africa, and the Middle East, opportunities will be missed, and indicators of what is emerging in the maritime domain, and how it will shape geopolitical narratives, will go unnoticed. In the last several decades, we have studied the Indian Ocean as a subset of South Asia, the Gulf, or Africa. Perhaps we can flip this perspective and view these coastlines as key sub-regions of the Indian Ocean and how they impact the Indian Ocean. So instead of looking out from land, we view the coastlines from the ocean in order to truly understand the connectivity, opportunity, challenges, and depth of issues in the maritime domain. Continental conflicts at the turn of this century ensured that the generations of foreign policymakers who rose up the ranks of their respective bureaucracies focused primarily on internal land borders. In the era of the Indo-Pacific, it is perhaps time to truly study the maritime domain and its complexities to understand the geopolitics of this new theater. This is to study the maritime domain as a core pillar of foreign policy.

The Indian Ocean as the theater for competition

Within the Indo-Pacific debate, there is much consideration, planning, and attention paid to the movements, developments, and trends across the Pacific. Much of this attention is tied to China and its activities in the region, with the perception that should there be a conflict (potentially a limited one), it would pan out in the wider Pacific. This view is particularly dominant as, in Washington's view, the Pacific is the key theater for competition with China. As a major player, Washington's views and priorities largely set the narrative of geopolitical priorities across the world. This is true of all big and superpowers; there is a reason history is often written by the victors. While the narrative of the potential for a conflict with China in the Pacific might be arguable, it is also true that neither Beijing, nor Washington, nor any of its allies or partners have the capacity or the intent to enter a conflict with the other. This pushes the conversation toward a long-drawn-out competition. In the context of a competition (not conflict), the Indian Ocean is likely to emerge as the key theater and the ocean where much of this competition will be decided.

The Indian Ocean is China's sea of vulnerabilities. Although Washington's Indian Ocean engagements post the Cold War have been focused on supporting its land-based conflicts in Asia and the Middle East, it does have better presence than Beijing. Moreover, the sheer number of players with more capacity today than during the Cold War, such as India, will significantly set the stage for competition in the Indian Ocean. Australia, France, Japan, South Korea, Singapore, Indonesia, Kenya, Mozambique, the UAE, Saudi Arabia, and Oman all have a growing dependency on the Indian Ocean through both trade and strategic interests. These nations also have a coastline in the Indian Ocean. Not all of them have the ability to command, cover, and respond to developments across the entire Indian Ocean. In this, the Indian Navy truly emerges as a key player, with both the intent and capacity to be able to maneuver and engage the different corners of the Indian Ocean. Still, the capacity to do so meaningfully is an ongoing policy debate within the Indian Navy and among India's policymakers.

So why would the Indian Ocean be the theater for competition when so much of the debate is focused on the Pacific? Chapters 3 and 4 go into detail in outlining the basis as well as the reasoning for this argument. Put simply, China has growing stakes in the Indian Ocean and limited capacity and capabilities to secure those interests. Beijing is not a resident power in the Indian Ocean, it has limited operational experience in this theater, and its major sea lines of communications are open to vulnerabilities and threat from many of its competitors and rivals, from India to the US. The Indian Ocean is also China's highway for its engagements with Africa, the Middle East, and Europe. If the Indian Ocean were inaccessible to China, its economic, diplomatic, and strategic interests and priorities would be impacted at a global scale. Chapter 3 discusses the importance of the Indian Ocean SLOCs to Beijing's energy security and its concerns beyond the Malacca dilemma. China will continue to pursue an ability to secure and advance its strategic and economic interests in the Indian Ocean. Over time, this will naturally involve military presence and support. As Beijing gradually seeks to address its geographical and operational disadvantages in the Indian Ocean, its competition with India, Australia, the US, Japan, and others will escalate. This is because Beijing is in some sort of a limited conflict for power with each of these nations, and has sovereignty disputes with India and Japan. Extending this competition from one theater to the other, say from land to the ocean for India, and from the East China Sea to the Indian Ocean for Japan, will catalyze the ongoing competition in the Indian Ocean. For Beijing, when it is truly able to secure its open vulnerabilities in the Indian Ocean, and to offer security to its emerging partnerships across the ocean, it will have an undeniable chance to emerge as global power.

The competition is set to be in the Indian Ocean. If Washington and its partners are looking for deterrence toolkits for the competition with Beijing, the Indian Ocean might hold many answers.

In understanding why and how the Indian Ocean impacts great power competition today, we must view the ocean as one continuous theater—which is a key argument of this book. This competition will be played out with Beijing, not only by Washington, Delhi, Canberra, Paris, and their friends and partners. This competition will be shaped very much by the actions, choices, priorities, and perceptions of smaller players, most importantly those of the island nations across the Indian Ocean. How the littoral nations view China's role in the Indian Ocean will, to a great extent, shape this competition. A first step in managing this competition might be to acknowledge that China is not a problematic player for many nations. Many players and nations will continue to seek deeper engagements with Beijing, inviting a greater Chinese presence across the Indian Ocean and thereby intensifying competition.

This ties the above observation—that many littorals and islands do not necessarily view China as a problematic player—to the argument that, as capitals across the Indo-Pacific manage their emerging competition with China, there is a need to shift perspectives and move toward understanding the concerns, views, and perceptions of its smaller neighbors, strategic partners, and the wider region. Geopolitical competition will no longer be defined by the choices of the bigger players alone.

Chapter 5 provides an answer to the above dilemma—where nations find themselves in a competition with China while their immediate neighbors, especially the island nations, continue to deepen their engagements with China. As Chapter 5 outlines, India, the US, Australia, Japan, France, and their partners would have to make some hard strategic choices to manage this security dilemma. If these maritime nations with a stake in the Indian Ocean utilize their island territories to respond to any growing security and military threat along the Indian Ocean chokepoints, they would have to adopt a dual approach of addressing military security through their island territories while focusing on issues of common security challenges with island nations. Common security challenges for the region include illegal fishing, natural disasters, and climate change policy, among others. Often categorized as "soft security issues" or "non-traditional security" issues, these issues nevertheless shape the larger security concerns of smaller nations, especially those of island nations. For a productive and meaningful engagement with island nations, it will be necessary to bring a sense of urgency to "non-traditional" security issues in the way smaller nations and island states do. Chapter 4 provides details of the importance of these issues and how they are perceived by island nations.

The underwater as the next domain

In looking ahead, the maritime domain is set to re-emerge as a decisive theater for power projection and competition in the twenty-first century. This has been true each time a new and emerging power set out to establish itself as a great or global power. Maritime power has been and remains central in a nation's ability to project their intentions, visions, ambitions, and goals. The twenty-first century, however, is distinctly different from previous eras of great power competition. The advance of technology has added a new dimension to competition and naval warfare. This is not limited to shipbuilding and advancing military capabilities. The role of technology in science and development will play an equal part in shaping the future of maritime security and great power competition.

The underwater domain is perhaps the least mapped domain in human history. We know more about space than we do about the depths of the ocean. This will be a contested region going forward. Ranging from the role of fishing vessels in strategic waters to underwater data centers, submarine cables, and deep-sea mining, developments and activities in the underwater domain will have a consequential impact for the projection of power. The underwater submarine cables that connect the world digitally and have allowed economic and technological advances are also new lines of communication. So far, we have mostly focused on sea power and sea denial through the significance of maritime chokepoints for SLOCs. The same logic would apply underwater for these new digital SLOCs and the need to protect them. Except the chokepoints and key centers for submarine cables will be different from those identified above the water surface detailed in Chapter 3. The advent of the internet is not new and nor are the submarine cables. But the threat of disruption and interests in them take the competition from the surface to the sub-surface level, a significantly difficult domain in which to maneuver. With increasing interest in deep-sea mining and under-water data centers, what does the road ahead look like for the under-water domain and warfighting? So far, for non-traditional security concerns such as illegal fishing and trafficking, the solutions remained above water. Now these challenges and non-traditional security threats are beginning to move into the underwater domain. Are we prepared to respond to those? Do we have enough knowledge of the underwater domain and how each of these issues interact with the others? Although I do not have an answer, or a suggested way forward in response to these questions, it will be important for policymakers, militaries, climate scientists, and researchers to study, explore, and determine their impact on and consequences for maritime security.

As a concluding thought for this book and this chapter, as the world entangles itself into a never-ending competition with the rise of China and its partners, a significant amount of military resources will be occupied in responding to non-traditional security issues. These issues range from maritime crime to illegal fishing, climate disasters, trafficking, search and rescue, and humanitarian missions. The manner in which we have thought about conflict, war, and geopolitics is beginning to change. In the maritime domain, these issues are intertwined and have consequential impacts; in terms of non-traditional as well as traditional security, and in terms of small nations potentially shaping great power competition. There is an urgent need to study the impact of maritime security right now. This book attempts to initiate some of these conversations, and put forward ideas and questions that will help in navigating this complex domain. I hope that in doing so, the book has helped to establish the importance of the Indian Ocean and its role in great power competi-tion in the twenty-first century.

Appendix

Overview of the Island Nations of the Indian Ocean (from east to west)

Country	Independence	Population	Language
Sri Lanka	4 February 1948 (from the UK)	22,889,201 (July 2020 est.)	Sinhala (official and national language) 87%, Tamil (official and national language) 28.5%, English 23.8% (2012 est.)
Maldives	26 July 1965 (from the UK)	391,904 (July 2020 est.)	Dhivehi (official, dialect of Sinhala, script derived from Arabic), English (spoken by most government officials)
Mauritius	March 1968 (from the UK)	1,379,365 (July 2020 est.)	Creole 86.5%, Bhojpuri 5.3%, French 4.1%, two languages 1.4%, other 2.6% (includes English, the official language of the National Assembly, which is spoken by less than 1% of the population), unspecified 0.1% (2011 est.)
Seychelles	29 June 1976 (from the UK)	95,981 (July 2020 est.)	Seychellois Creole (official) 89.1%, English (official) 5.1%, French (official) 0.7%, other 3.8%, unspecified 1.4% (2010 est.)
Madagascar	26 June 1960 (from France)	26,955,737 (July 2020 est.)	French (official), Malagasy (official), English
Comoros	6 July 1975 (from France)	846,281 (July 2020 est.)	Arabic (official), French (official), Shikomoro (official; a blend of Swahili and Arabic) (Comorian)

Source: "The World Factbook," CIA, 2020, https://www.cia.gov/the-world-factbook/.

Notes

1 Introduction

1. Sugata Bose, *A Hundred Horizons: The Indian Ocean in the Age of Global Empire* (London and Cambridge, MA: Harvard University Press, 2006).
2. Rory Medcalf, "The Indo-Pacific: What's in a name?" *The American Interest* 9, no. 2 (October 2013), https://www.the-american-interest.com/2013/10/10/the-indo-pacific-whats-in-a-name/.
3. "World oil transit chokepoints," US Energy Information Administration, July 25, 2017, https://www.eia.gov/international/analysis/special-topics/World_Oil_Transit_Chokepoints.
4. "Maritime chokepoints are critical to global energy security," in Today in Energy, US Energy Information Administration, August 1, 2017, https://www.eia.gov/todayinenergy/detail.php?id=32292.
5. Ashley Jackson, *War and Empire in Mauritius and the Indian Ocean* (London: Palgrave Macmillan, 2001).
6. Roger Crowley, *Conquerors: How Portugal Forged the First Global Empire* (London: Faber & Faber, 2015).
7. Jackson, *War and Empire in Mauritius and the Indian Ocean*; Ashley Jackson, *Of Islands, Ports and Sea Lanes: Africa and the Indian Ocean in the Second World War* (Warwick: Helion, 2018).
8. Sergei DeSilva-Ranasinghe, "Why the Indian Ocean matters," *The Diplomat*, March 2, 2011. https://thediplomat.com/2011/03/why-the-indian-ocean-matters/.
9. World Wildlife Fund Report, *Unregulated Fishing on the High Seas of the Indian Ocean: The Impact on, Risk to, and Challenges for Sustainable Fishing and Ocean Health* (Brussels: WWF, 2020), https://wwfeu.awsassets.panda.org/downloads/wwftmt_unregulated_fishing_on_the_high_seas_of_the_indian_ocean_2020.pdf.
10. Indian Ocean Tuna Commission, Food and Agriculture Organization of the United Nations, *Status summary for species of Tuna and Tuna-like species under the IOTC Fisheries*, 2021. https://www.fao.org/fishery/en/collection/iotc_ssr.

11. "AIS (Automatic Identification System) overview," NATO Shipping Center, https://shipping.nato.int/nsc/operations/news/2021/ais-automatic-identification-system-overview; https://globalfishingwatch.org/faqs/what-is-ais/#:~:text=1,in%20order%20to%20avoid%20collisions.

12. Robert D. Kaplan, *The Revenge of Geography: What the Map Tells Us about Coming Conflicts and the Battle against Fate* (New York: Random House, 2012), p. 83.

13. Robert D. Kaplan, *Monsoon: The Indian Ocean and the Future of American Power* (New York: Random House, 2010), pp. 9–12.

14. Ibid., pp. 9–12.

15. Michael Pearson, *The Indian Ocean* (London: Routledge, 2003), p. 21.

16. Sophie Blanchy, "A matrilineal and matrilocal Muslim society in flux: Negotiating gender and family relations in the Comoros," *Africa* 89, no. 1 (February 2019): 21–39.

2 The Cold War, the Special Relationship, and Diego Garcia

1. Kent E. Calder, *Embattled Garrison: Comparative Base Politics and American Globalism* (Princeton, NJ: Princeton University Press, 2008).

2. K.M. Panikkar, "The British lake," in *India and the Indian Ocean* (London: George Allen & Unwin, 1945), ch. 6.

3. Robert Komer, "Memorandum from the President's Deputy Special Assistant for National Security Affairs (Komer) to the President's Special Assistant for National Security Affairs (Bundy) and Francis Bator of the National Security Council Staff," US Department of State: Office of the Historian, Washington, January 26, 1966, https://history.state.gov/historicaldocuments/frus1964-68v21/d41.

4. Ibid.

5. Ibid.

6. Joint Chiefs of Staff, "Memorandum for the Secretary of Defense, subject: Indian Ocean islands," US Department of State: Office of the Historian, Washington, May 20, 1965. Note, all dollar figures given in this book are USD.

7. Joint Chiefs of Staff, "Memorandum from the Joint Chiefs of Staff to Secretary of Defense McNamara," US Department of State: Office of the Historian, Washington, July 25, 1967, https://history.state.gov/historicaldocuments/frus-964-68v21/d45.

8. Ibid.

9. Ibid.

10. Allan Ngari and Clive Baldwin, "Let Chagossians go home, decide their future," Human Rights Watch, June 21, 2023, https://www.hrw.org/news/2023/06/21/let-chagossians-go-home-decide-their-future.

11. Joint Chiefs of Staff, "Memorandum from the Joint Chiefs of Staff to Secretary of Defense McNamara," US Department of State: Office of the Historian, Washington, July 25, 1967, https://history.state.gov/historicaldocuments/frus-964-68v21/d45.

12. Robert S. McNamara, "Memorandum from Secretary of Defense McNamara to the Secretary of the Navy (Ignatius)," US Department of State: Office of the

Historian, Washington, October 27, 1967, https://history.state.gov/historical-documents/frus1964-68v21/d46.

13. Ibid.

14. Joint Chiefs of Staff, "Memorandum from the Joint Chiefs of Staff to Secretary of Defense McNamara," US Department of State: Office of the Historian, Washington, April 10, 1968, https://history.state.gov/historicaldocuments/frus1964-68v21/d47.

15. Ibid.

16. Ibid.

17. Ibid.

18. Paul H. Nitze, "Memorandum from the Deputy Secretary of Defense (Nitze)," US Department of State: Office of the Historian, Washington, June 15, 1968, https://history.state.gov/historicaldocuments/frus1964-68v21/d48.

19. The Kagnew Station was completely closed when the last Americans left on April 29, 1977.

20. Ibid.

21. Dean Rusk, "Telegram from the Department of State to the Embassy in the United Kingdom," US Department of State: Office of the Historian, Washington, July 3, 1968, 1912Z, https://history.state.gov/historicaldocuments/frus1964-68v21/d49.

22. David K.E. Bruce, "Telegram from the Embassy in the United Kingdom to the Department of State," US Department of State, London, September 4, 1968, 1037Z, https://history.state.gov/historicaldocuments/frus1964-68v21/d50.

23. Ibid.

24. Ibid.

25. Thomas Hinman Moorer, "Paper Prepared in the Office of the Chief of Naval Operations (Moorer)," US Department of State: Office of the Historian, Washington, February 11, 1970, https://history.state.gov/historicaldocuments/frus1969-76v24/d39.

26. Ibid.

27. Ibid.

28. Ibid.

29. Ibid.

30. Ibid.

31. "Editorial note," US Department of State: Office of the Historian, Washington, November 25, 1970, https://history.state.gov/historicaldocuments/frus1969-76v24/d44.

32. Harry A. Bergold, Jr., "Memorandum from the Deputy Assistant Secretary of Defense for European and NATO Affairs (Bergold) to the Deputy Assistant Secretary of Defense for Security Assistance (Peet)," US Department of State: Office of the Historian, Washington, January 17, 1974, https://history.state.gov/historicaldocuments/frus1969-76ve08/d65.

33. "Editorial note," US Department of State: Office of the Historian, Washington, October 3, 1970, https://history.state.gov/historicaldocuments/frus1969-76v24/d41.

34. Ibid.

35. Henry Kissinger, "National Security Study Memorandum 199: Indian Ocean Strategy," National Security Council of the USA, Washington, March 14, 1974,

https://www.nixonlibrary.gov/sites/default/files/virtuallibrary/documents/nssm/nssm_199.pdf, refers to the "prospective opening of the Suez canal . . ." which was blocked from 1967 to 1975 during the Arab–Israeli wars. It also refers to the period 1971–75 in the past tense.

36. "Indian Ocean Strategy (Response to NSSM 199)," National Security Council of the USA, Washington, https://2001-2009.state.gov/documents/organization/97480.pdf.

37. Henry A. Kissinger, "National Security Study Memorandum 104", National Security Council of the USA, Washington, November 9, 1970, https://history.state.gov/historicaldocuments/frus1969-76v24/d42

38. Henry Kissinger, "National Security Study Memorandum 199: Indian Ocean Strategy," National Security Council of the USA, Washington, March 14, 1974, https://www.nixonlibrary.gov/sites/default/files/virtuallibrary/documents/nssm/nssm_199.pdf.

39. Ibid.

40. Operation Enduring Freedom was a response to attacks in the US on September 11, 2001.

3 Chokepoints and Naval Competition

1. "Study Prepared in Response to National Security Study Memorandum 199: US IOR Strategy 1976," US Department of State: Office of the Historian, Washington, undated, https://history.state.gov/historicaldocuments/frus1969-76ve08/d77.

2. H.E. Mr. Shinzo Abe, "Speech to the Parliament of the Republic of India: Confluence of the two seas," Ministry of Foreign Affairs of Japan, August 22, 2007, https://www.mofa.go.jp/region/asia-paci/pmv0708/speech-2.html.

3. Lee Cordner, "Rethinking maritime security in the Indian Ocean region," *Journal of the Indian Ocean Region* 6, no. 1 (2010): 67–85.

4. Milan Vego, "Strategic framework," in *Maritime Strategy and Seas Control: Theory and Practice* (New York: Routledge, 2016), p. 21.

5. Milan Vego, "Sea control and sea denial," in *Naval Strategy and Operation in Narrow Seas* (London: Routledge, 1999).

6. Vego, "Strategic framework," p. 24.

7. Ibid., p. 26.

8. Ibid., p. 188.

9. Monoranjan Bezboruah, *US Strategy in the Indian Ocean: The International Response* (Westport, CT: Praeger, 1977), p. 6.

10. Milan Vego, "Admiral John Fisher in chokepoint control," in *Maritime Strategy and Seas Control*, p. 188.

11. Ibid., p. 193.

12. "World oil transit chokepoints," US Energy Information Administration, July 25, 2017.

13. Ibid.

14. Ibid.

15. Ibid.

16. "The Strait of Hormuz is the world's most important oil transit chokepoint," US Energy Information Administration, June 20, 2019.

17. "World oil transit chokepoints," US Energy Information Administration, July 25, 2017; "The Strait of Hormuz is the world's most important oil transit chokepoint," US Energy Information Administration, June 20, 2019.

18. "Today in energy," US Energy Information Administration, December 27, 2019, https://www.eia.gov/todayinenergy/detail.php?id=42338.

19. "World oil transit chokepoints," US Energy Information Administration, July 25, 2017.

20. "Why the Suez Canal," Suez Canal Authority, 2019, https://www.suezcanal.gov. eg/English/About/Pages/WhySuezCanal.aspx.

21. Rick Gladstone and Megan Specia, "What to know about the Suez Canal and the cargo ship that was stuck there," *The New York Times*, updated January 1, 2022, https://www.nytimes.com/2021/03/25/world/middleeast/suez-canal-container-ship.html.

22. Aaron Clark, "Suez snarl seen halting $9.6 billion a day of ship traffic," *Bloomberg News*, March 25, 2021, https://www.bloomberg.com/news/articles/2021-03-25/suez-snarl-seen-halting-9-6-billion-a-day-worth-of-ship-traffic.

23. "Map: The strategic importance of the Indian Ocean," Carnegie Endowment for International Peace, September 2022, https://carnegieendowment.org/publications/interactive/indian-ocean-map/?page=Application---The-Strategic-Importance-of-the-Indian-Ocean.

24. You Ji, "Dealing with the Malacca dilemma: China's efforts to protect its energy supply," *Strategic Analysis* 31, no. 3 (2007): 467–89.

25. "China: Executive summary," US Energy Information Administration, August 8, 2022, https://www.eia.gov/international/analysis/country/CHN.

26. These numbers could change in 2023–4 based on the ongoing war in Ukraine.

27. "China: Executive summary," US Energy Information Administration, August 8, 2022, https://www.eia.gov/international/analysis/country/CHN.

28. Darshana M. Baruah, Nitya Labh, and Jessica Greely, *Mapping the Indian Ocean Region*, Report, Washington, DC: Carnegie Endowment for International Peace, June 2023, https://carnegieendowment.org/2023/06/15/mapping-indian-ocean-region-pub-89971.

29. Office of the Secretary of Defense, *Annual Report to Congress: Military and Security Developments Involving the People's Republic of China*, US Department of Defense, https://media.defense.gov/2021/Nov/03/2002885874/-1/-1/0/2021-CMPR-FINAL.PDF.

30. Darshana M. Baruah, "Testimony. Surrounding the ocean: PRC influence in the Indian Ocean," US House of Representatives Committee on Foreign Affairs, April 18, 2023, https://docs.house.gov/meetings/FA/FA05/20230418/115667/HHRG-118-FA05-Wstate-BaruahD-20230418.pdf.

31. Hu Bo, *Chinese Maritime Power in the 21st Century* (London: Routledge, 2020).

32. "The Indian Ocean Strategic Map, Regional Trade," Indian Ocean Initiative, Carnegie Endowment for International Peace, 2023, https://carnegieendowment.org/publications/interactive/indian-ocean-map/?page=Economy.

33. Ibid.

34. Baruah et al., *Mapping the Indian Ocean Region*; "The Indian Ocean Strategic Map, Regional Trade."

35. Samuel Bashfield, "Mauritian sovereignty over the Chagos Archipelago? Strategic implications for Diego Garcia from a UK–US perspective," *Journal of the Indian Ocean Region* 16 (2020): 166–81.

36. Darshana M. Baruah, "Showing up is half the battle: US maritime forces in the Indian Ocean," *War on the Rocks*, March 18, 2021, https://warontherocks.com/2021/03/showing-up-is-half-the-battle-u-s-maritime-forces-in-the-indian-ocean/.

37. David Scott, "Britain returns to the Indian Ocean," *Commonwealth Journal of International Affairs* 107 (2018): 307–16.

4 Island Nations' Agency and Great Power Competition

1. Abdulla Shahid, "Why small island states are vulnerable but not powerless," Carnegie Endowment for International Peace, September 27, 2022, https://carnegieendowment.org/2022/09/27/why-small-island-states-are-vulnerable-but-not-powerless-pub-88015.

2. Baruah et al., *Mapping the Indian Ocean Region.*

3. John F. Bradford, "The maritime strategy of the United States: Implications for Indo-Pacific sea lanes," *Contemporary Southeast Asia* 33, no. 2 (2011): 183–208, http://www.jstor.org/stable/41288826.

4. Kallol Bhattacherjee, "Kissinger, Nixon 'helped' Pakistan in 1971, documents from US archive reveal," *The Hindu*, December 1, 2023, https://www.thehindu.com/news/national/kissinger-nixon-broke-us-rule-to-help-pakistan-sent-aircraft-from-third-countries-as-they-feared-india-was-about-to-attack-west-pakistan/article67591823.ece.

5. C. Raja Mohan and Darshana M. Baruah, "Deepening the India–France maritime partnership," Carnegie Endowment for International Peace, February 26, 2018, https://carnegieendowment.org/files/Mohan_Baruah_Deepening_The_India_France_Maritime_Partnership.pdf.

6. Nithyani Anandakuan, "The Sri Lankan civil war and its history, revisited in 2020," *Harvard International Review*, August 31, 2020, https://hir.harvard.edu/sri-lankan-civil-war/.

7. Darshana M. Baruah, "The three things the United States must do at its historic Pacific Islands Summit," Carnegie Endowment for International Peace, September 28, 2022, https://carnegieendowment.org/2022/09/28/three-things-united-states-must-do-at-its-historic-pacific-islands-summit-pub-88033.

8. James McBride, Noah Berman, and Andrew Chatzky, "China's massive Belt and Road Initiative," Council on Foreign Relations, February 2, 2023, https://www.cfr.org/backgrounder/chinas-massive-belt-and-road-initiative.

9. Michael J. Green, *China's Maritime Silk Road: Strategic and Economic Implications for the Indo-Pacific Region*, Washington, DC: Center for Strategic and International Studies, April 2, 2018, https://www.csis.org/analysis/chinas-maritime-silk-road-strategic-and-economic-implications-indo-pacific-region.

10. Ibid.

11. Maria Abi-Habib, "How China got Sri Lanka to cough up a port," *The New York Times*, June 25, 2018, https://www.nytimes.com/2018/06/25/world/asia/china-sri-lanka-port.html.

12. Lee Jones and Shahar Hameiri, "Debunking the myth of debt-trap diplomacy," Chatham House, August 19, 2020, https://www.chathamhouse.org/2020/08/debunking-myth-debt-trap-diplomacy; Shahar Hameiri, "Debunking the myth of China's debt trap diplomacy," *The Interpreter*, September 9, 2020, https://www.lowyinstitute.org/the-interpreter/debunking-myth-china-s-debt-trap-diplomacy.

13. Deep Pal, "China's influence in South Asia: Vulnerabilities and resilience in four countries," Carnegie Endowment for International Peace, October 13, 2021, https://carnegieendowment.org/2021/10/13/china-s-influence-in-south-asia-vulnerabilities-and-resilience-in-four-countries-pub-85552.

14. Deborah Brautigam and Meg Rithmire, "The Chinese debt trap is a myth," *The Atlantic*, February 6, 2021, https://www.theatlantic.com/international/archive/2021/02/china-debt-trap-diplomacy/617953/.

15. This section is based primarily on the author's interviews with officials from island nations across the Indian Ocean. The author traveled to Sri Lanka, the Maldives, Mauritius, Madagascar, and Comoros between 2017 and 2020 to better understand island perspectives. This section aims to bring to the foreground the sentiments and views of island nations, without offering a counterpoint. There is plenty of literature discussing the views of bigger powers and their engagements with island nations. This section, drawn from interviews on the islands and through conferences, aims to provide the islands' perspective on Indian Ocean developments. It is an attempt to highlight island agency and how it is impacting great power competition. The interviews were with officials from ministries of foreign affairs, national security councils, prime minister's offices, navy and defense officials, and departments of tourism and development. Many of the perspectives are direct quotes but the majority of the officials requested not to be identified. They were aware of the author's intention to write a book and wanted to share frank conversations so the book could present this perspective without identifying the office or the official. This was a common theme the author heard across all islands. A planned visit to Seychelles was disrupted by the 2020 coronavirus pandemic, but the author was able to interview and speak with officials and experts from the island nation virtually and through conferences.

16. "Sri Lanka China relations," Embassy of the Democratic Socialist Republic of Sri Lanka, https://www.beijing.embassy.gov.lk/srirelation.

17. "Ambassador of Union of Comoros to China: Mining town inspires young people in Comoros," *People's Daily Overseas Edition*, August 9, 2022, https://eng.yidaiyilu.gov.cn/p/267461.html.

18. Darshana M. Baruah, "India in the Indo-Pacific: New Delhi's theater of opportunity," Carnegie Endowment for International Peace, June 30, 2020, https://carnegieendowment.org/2020/06/30/india-in-indo-pacific-new-delhi-s-theater-of-opportunity-pub-82205.

19. Based on interviews conducted by the author in February 2020.

20. Robert A. Manning and Bharath Gopalaswamy, "Is Abdulla Yameen handing over the Maldives to China?," *Foreign Policy*, March 21, 2018, https://foreignpolicy.com/2018/03/21/is-abdulla-yameen-handing-over-the-maldives-to-china/; Sam Meredith, "Trouble in paradise: All you need to know about the Maldives' ongoing political crisis," *CNBC*, February 8, 2018, https://www.cnbc.

com/2018/02/08/maldives-crisis-all-you-need-to-know-about-the-political-turmoil.html; Nayma Qayum, "The crisis in the Maldives, explained," *The Washington Post*, February 12, 2018, https://www.washingtonpost.com/news/monkey-cage/wp/2018/02/12/how-is-trade-with-china-related-to-the-state-of-emergency-in-maldives-heres-what-you-need-to-know/; Sunaina Kumar and Angela Stanzel, "The Maldives crisis and the China–India chess match," *The Diplomat*, March 15, 2018, https://thediplomat.com/2018/03/the-maldives-crisis-and-the-china-india-chess-match/.

21. Based on interviews conducted by the author in February 2020.
22. Based on interviews conducted by the author in February 2020.
23. Based on interviews conducted by the author in September 2019.
24. Yarno Ritzen, "Evidence points to secret Indian Navy base on Mauritian island," *Al-Jazeera*, August 3, 2021, https://www.aljazeera.com/news/2021/8/3/evidence-points-to-secret-indian-navy-base-on-mauritian-island.
25. Based on interviews conducted by the author in December 2017.
26. Nayanima Basu, "Show gratitude to India, Mauritius PM tells oppn as Agalega Island row adds to snooping fire," *The Print*, July 29, 2022, https://theprint.in/diplomacy/show-gratitude-to-india-mauritius-pm-tells-oppn-as-agalega-island-row-adds-to-snooping-fire/1060764/.
27. David Vine, *Island of Shame: The Secret History of the US Military Base on Diego Garcia* (Princeton, NJ: Princeton University Press, 2009).
28. Speech by Amb. Koonjul at Ocean Nations: An Indo-Pacific Islands Dialogue, September 19–20, 2021, New York, https://carnegieendowment.org/2021/09/20/ocean-nations-indo-pacific-islands-dialogue-event-7680.
29. Based on interviews conducted by the author in December 2017.
30. "Mayotte votes for full French integration," *France24*, March 29, 2009, https://www.france24.com/en/20090329-mayotte-votes-full-french-integration-.
31. It is worth noting that the Covid pandemic perhaps played a significant role in shifting trade and economic patterns for many nations. Given the time it takes to report data and the number of years it takes before a shift in trends can be captured, it is unlikely we will see the impact and implications of Covid for trade partners in the data currently reported.
32. A.J.G. Simoes and C.A. Hidalgo, "The Economic Complexity Observatory: An analytical tool for understanding the dynamics of economic development," 2011, https://oec.world/en/resources/about.
33. Based on interviews conducted by the author in October 2019.
34. Based on interviews conducted by the author in October 2019.
35. Based on interviews conducted by the author in October 2019.
36. "The Indian Ocean Strategic Map," Carnegie Endowment for International Peace, 2023, https://carnegieendowment.org/publications/interactive/indian-ocean-map/.
37. Dipanjan Roy Chaudhury, "India, France explore 3rd country projects in Western Indian Ocean region," *The Economic Times,* October 24, 2019, https://economictimes.indiatimes.com/news/defence/india-france-explore-3rd-country-projects-in-western-indian-ocean-region/articleshow/71743985.cms?from=mdr.
38. Based on interviews conducted by the author in September 2019.

39. "Mapping oil and gas contracts in the northern Mozambique Channel," World Wildlife Fund, https://wwf-sight.org/mapping-oil-and-gas-concessions-in-northern-mozambique-channel/.
40. Based on interviews conducted by the author in September 2019.
41. Darshana M. Baruah, "View: African islands in the Indian Ocean—Looking beyond Delhi's strategic blindness," *The Economic Times*, October 17, 2019, https://economictimes.indiatimes.com/news/defence/view-african-islands-in-the-indian-ocean-looking-beyond-delhis-strategic-blindness/articleshow/71627802.cms.
42. Lt. Said Lavani, Regional Maritime Information Fusion Center, November 11, 2022, https://dcoc.org/wp-content/uploads/LAVAN-COMOROS-Presentation-of-RMIFC.pdf.

5 Island Territories: Beyond an Unsinkable Aircraft Carrier

1. K.M. Panikkar, *India and the Indian Ocean* (Crows Nest: Allen & Unwin, 1951).
2. R.V.R. Murthy, *Andaman and Nicobar Islands: Development and Decentralization* (New Delhi: Mittal Publication, 2005), p. 20.
3. Clare Anderson et al., *New Histories of the Andaman Islands: Landscape, Place and Identity in the Bay of Bengal, 1790–2012* (Cambridge: Cambridge University Press, 2016).
4. Marco Polo, *The Travels of Marco Polo: The Complete Yule-Cordier Edition* (New York: Dover Publications, 1920), p. 306.
5. Ibid., p. 309.
6. Junjiro Takakusu, "An introduction to I-tsing's Record of Buddhist religion as practised in India and the Malay Archipelago (AD 671–695)" (PhD diss., Oxford University, 1896), pp. 30–31, https://jscholarship.library.jhu.edu/bitstream/handle/1774.2/36242/31151010016214.pdf.
7. Aparna Vaidik, *Imperial Andamans: Colonial Encounter and Island History* (London: Palgrave Macmillan, 2010), pp. 17–18.
8. Ibid., p. 20.
9. Anthropological Survey of India, Ministry of Culture, Government of India, https://ansi.gov.in/regional-centre-andaman-niccobar/.
10. Hermann Kulke et al., *Nagapattinam to Suvarnadwipa: Reflections on the Chola Naval Expeditions to Southeast Asia* (Singapore: Institute of Southeast Asian Studies, 2009).
11. Ibid., pp. 76–91.
12. Michael Snyder, "Kanhoji Angre: India's first naval commander," Gateway House, September 4, 2012, https://www.gatewayhouse.in/kanhoji-angre-indias-first-naval-commander/.
13. Sanat Kaul, *Andaman and Nicobar Islands: India's Untapped Strategic Assets* (New Delhi: Pentagon Press, 2015), pp. 28–36; Anderson et. al, *New Histories of the Andaman Islands.*
14. Vaidik, *Imperial Andamans*, pp. 5–9.
15. Ibid., pp. 16–34.
16. Ibid., p. 37.
17. Ibid., p. 13.

18. Frederic John Mouat, "Narrative of an expedition to the Andaman Islands in 1857," *Journal of the Royal Geographical Society of London*, 32 (London, 1862): 109–126; Vaidik, *Imperial Andamans*, p. 179.
19. The *Senshi Sosho* is the official World War II history of Imperial Japan. The series was compiled by the History Department of the Ministry of Defense, Japan. The series was published between 1966 and 1980 and consists of 102 volumes, of which 21 volumes are on the navy. Many documents and plans were destroyed by Imperial Japan at the time of the surrender to the US in 1945. The series is built on documents (journals, notes, maps), which were taken and eventually returned by the US. The team tasked with creating the series collected personal journals and notes as well as interviewing veterans of the war. Although the *Senshi Sosho* series was undertaken by the Japanese Ministry of Defense, it was first published privately by Asagumo Shimbunsha. Currently only two volumes have been translated into English. This chapter refers to the translation of vol. 26, *Second Senshi Sosho Volume: The Operations of the Navy in the Dutch East Indies and the Bay of Bengal*, War History Office of the National Defense College of Japan, translated by Willem Remmelink (Leiden: Leiden University Press, 2018).
20. Ibid.
21. Ibid., pp. 565–658.
22. Morton H. Halperin, *The 1958 Taiwan Straits Crisis: A Documented History* (Santa Monica, CA: RAND Corporation, 1966), https://www.rand.org/pubs/research_memoranda/RM4900.html.
23. Edward S. Miller, *War Plan Orange: The US Strategy to Defeat Japan 1897–1945* (Annapolis, MD: Naval Institute Press, 1991), p. 33.
24. Ibid., p. 33.
25. Ibid., p. 87.
26. Ibid., p. 87.
27. Samuel E. Morison, *The Two-Ocean War: A Short History of the United States Navy in the Second World War* (Boston, MA: Little, Brown, 1963), p. 283.
28. Sadao Asada, *From Mahan to Pearl Harbor: The Imperial Japanese Navy in the United States* (Annapolis, MD: Naval Institute Press, 2006), pp. 12–13, 22.
29. Morison, *The Two-Ocean War*, p. 282.
30. Vaidik, *Imperial Andamans*.
31. Vice Admiral M.P. Muralidharan, "Economic and strategic importance of sea in modern Indian context," *Indian Defense Review*, February 28, 2019, http://www.indiandefencereview.com/spotlights/economic-and-strategic-importance-of-sea-in-modern-indian-context/.
32. Vice Admiral Gulab Mohanlal Hiranandani, *Transition to Triumph: History of the Indian Navy, 1965–1975* (New Delhi: Lance Publishers, 2000), p. 35.
33. Ibid., p. 470; Kaul, *Andaman and Nicobar Islands*.
34. Hiranandani, *Transition to Triumph*, p. 470.
35. Admiral B.S. Soman was the fourth chief of naval staff, India, between 1962 and 1966.
36. Rear Admiral Satyindra Singh, *Blueprint to Bluewater: The Indian Navy 1951–65* (New Delhi: Lance Publishers, 1992).
37. Ibid., p. 458.

38. Ibid., p. 458.
39. Ibid., p. 459.
40. Ibid., p. 459.
41. Ibid., p. 458.
42. Ibid., p. 458; Yogesh Joshi, "Sailing through the Cold War: Indian Navy quest for a submarine arm, 1947–67," *India Review*, 17, no. 5 (2018): 492–4.
43. Hiranandani, *Transition to Triumph*, p. 85.
44. Ibid., p. 185.
45. Ibid., p. 185.
46. Srinath Raghavan, *1971: A Global History of the Creation of Bangladesh* (Cambridge, MA: Harvard University Press, 2013).
47. Hiranandani, *Transition to Triumph*, p. 184.
48. Ibid., p. 184.
49. Ibid., p. 191.
50. Ibid., p. 184; Himanil Rana, "Missing in action: India's aircraft carriers," *The Interpreter*, Lowy Institute, October 11, 2018, https://www.lowyinstitute.org/the-interpreter/missing-action-india-aircraft-carriers.
51. Admiral Arun Prakash was the Indian chief of naval staff (CNS) between 2004 and 2006.
52. Arun Prakash, "Evolution of the Indian Navy: Towards a 'maritime awakening'?", in Harsh V. Pant, ed., *The Routledge Handbook of Indian Defence Policy: Themes, Structures and Doctrines* (New Delhi: Routledge, 2020).
53. Hiranandani, *Transition to Triumph*.
54. Anit Mukherjee, "India's Joint Andaman and Nicobar Command is a failed experiment," *Asia Pacific Bulletin, East-West Center*, November 17, 2015, https://www.eastwestcenter.org/system/tdf/private/apb289.pdf?file=1&type=node&id=34843
55. *From Surprise to Reckoning: The Kargil Review Committee Report* (New Delhi: Sage Publications), December 15, 1999.
56. *Kargil Committee Report: An Appraisal*, https://archive.claws.in/images/journals_doc/1400824637Report%20of%20the%20Kargil%20Review%20Committee%20%20CJ%20SSummer%202009.pdf.
57. *From Surprise to Reckoning: The Kargil Review Committee Report*, 1999.
58. Based on author's interview with a former foreign secretary, New Delhi, November 29, 2019.
59. Ibid.
60. Kaul, *Andaman and Nicobar Islands*, p. 7.
61. Based on the author's interview with a former deputy national security advisor. New Delhi, December 3, 2019.
62. Kaul, *Andaman and Nicobar Islands*.
63. India State of Forest Report 2017, https://fsi.nic.in/isfr2017/andaman-nocobar-island-isfr-2017.pdf. On environmental concerns, see "State Action Plan on Climate Change," Ministry of Environment, Forest, and Climate Change, November, 2013, http://moef.gov.in/wp-content/uploads/2017/08/Andaman-and-Nicobar.pdf.
64. Andaman and Nicobar Islands, Ministry of Tribal Affairs, https://tribal.nic.in/notificationAndaman.aspx. To understand the indigenous tribes of the islands from an anthropological point of view, see Sudipto Sengupta, "Madhumala

Chattopadhaya, the woman who made the Sentinelese put their arrows down," *The Print*, November 29, 2018, https://theprint.in/opinion/madhumala-chattopadhyay-the-woman-who-made-the-sentinelese-put-their-arrows-down/156330/; see also S. Venkatanarayanan, "Protect indigenous people," *The Hindu*, November 29, 2018, https://www.thehindu.com/opinion/op-ed/protect-indigenous-people/article25616520.ece and "Andamans: US man's death puts spotlight on tribal tourism," *BBC News*, November 23, 2018, https://www.bbc.com/news/world-asia-india-46313965.

65. Kaul, *Andaman and Nicobar Islands*, pp. 18–24.

66. Centre for Coastal Zone Management and Coastal Shelter Belt, Ministry of Environment, Forests and Climate Change, Government of India, http://iomenvis.nic.in/index2.aspx?slid=60&sublinkid=25&langid=1&mid=1.

67. International Solar Alliance, https://isolaralliance.org.

68. "Prime Minister's speech at the East Asia Summit," Ministry of External Affairs, Government of India, November 4, 2019, https://www.mea.gov.in/Speeches-Statements.htm?dtl/32171/Prime_Ministers_Speech_at_the_East_Asia_Summit_04_November_2019.

69. Darshana M. Baruah, "Sister islands in the Indian Ocean region: Linking the Andaman and Nicobar Islands to La Réunion," *War on the Rocks*, March 20, 2019, https://warontherocks.com/2019/03/sister-islands-in-the-indian-ocean-region-linking-the-andaman-and-nicobar-islands-to-la-reunion/.

70. On Japan, see Ministry of Defense, https://www.mod.go.jp/e/publ/w_paper/2019.html; https://www.japantimes.co.jp/news/2019/03/26/national/politics-diplomacy/gsdf-launches-bases-kagoshima-okinawa-defense-japans-southwestern-islands/, and Michael MacArthur Bosack, "Understanding Japan's southwest islands buildup," *The Japan Times*, April 22, 2019, https://www.japantimes.co.jp/opinion/2019/04/22/commentary/japan-commentary/understanding-japans-southwest-islands-buildup/. For an overview of Japan's strategy and doctrine see Alessio Patalano, "Japan as a seapower: Strategy, doctrine, and capabilities under three defence reviews, 1995–2010," *Journal of Strategic Studies* 37 (2014), https://www.tandfonline.com/doi/abs/10.1080/01402390.2014.904788?src=recsys&journalCode=fjss20.

71. Based on the author's interactions and conversations with Japanese Air and Maritime Self Defense Forces in Airbase Naha, Okinawa, August 2018. Similar author interactions with officials in the US INDOPACOM and civil authorities in Hawaii, August 27–31, 2019.

72. Based on the author's interview with a former commander-in-chief of the Maritime Self-Defense Force, Japan, September 11, 2019. For more information on Japan's lessons from World War II on island defense, see the keynote address by Yoji Koda, "Island defense and seizure operations, and naval strategic lessons learned by Imperial Japan in the Pacific theater of operations during World War II," International Forum on War History, September 25, 2013, http://www.nids.mod.go.jp/english/event/forum/pdf/2013/02.pdf.

73. The Command is responsible for logistics and infrastructure, including island defense on US bases in South Korea, Okinawa, and Guam.

74. Based on the author's interview with an official at Camp Butler, Marine Corps Installation Pacific, Okinawa, Japan. January 3, 2020.

75. Joshua T. White, "China's Indian Ocean ambition: Investment, influence, and military advantage," Brookings Institution, June 2020, https://www.brookings.edu/research/chinas-indian-ocean-ambitions/.

76. Based on the author's interactions with military officials and civil authorities in Port Blair, February 20–22, 2017. The author has also interacted with officials at the HQ Integrated Defence Staff (IDS) and with retired military and civilian officials tasked with such reports in 2017 and 2018.

77. Based on the author's interaction and conversations at the Office of the Chief Secretary, Port Blair. February 20, 2017.

78. Jyotika Sood and Utpal Bhaskar, "Eye on China, India plans infrastructure boost in Andaman and Nicobar islands," *LiveMint*, June 26, 2017, https://www.livemint.com/Politics/TDQmSWIJKb8CazbITu0tCN/Eye-on-China-India-plans-infrastructure-boost-in-Andaman-an.html; Dinakar Peri, "Navy's new air base in north of Port Blair," *The Hindu*, January 7, 2019, https://www.thehindu.com/news/national/navys-new-air-base-in-north-of-port-blair/article25934644.ece.

79. Rajat Arora, "Modi government's 10,000 crore plan to transform Andaman and Nicobar islands," *The Economic Times*, June 26, 2015, https://economictimes.indiatimes.com/news/economy/infrastructure/modi-governments-rs-10000-crore-plan-to-transform-andaman-and-nicobar-islands/articleshow/4911 1067.cms.

80. "Incredible islands of India (holistic development)," NITI Aayog, https://niti.gov.in/writereaddata/files/document_publication/IslandsDev.pdf.

81. "Shri Amit Shah chairs meeting of the Island Development Agency focusing on green development in the islands to reach a new height," Press Information Bureau, Ministry of Home Affairs, Government of India, January 13, 2020, https://pib.gov.in/Pressreleaseshare.aspx?PRID=1599301.

82. "Andaman & Nicobar can be springboard for India's Look East policy," *The Economic Times*, January 11, 2014, https://economictimes.indiatimes.com/news/politics-and-nation/andaman-nicobar-can-be-springboard-for-indias-look-east-policy-pranab-mukherjee/articleshow/28686775.cms?from=mdr; Pushpita Das, "Securing the Andaman and Nicobar Islands," *Journal of Strategic Analysis* 35 (2011), https://www.tandfonline.com/doi/full/10.1080/09700161.2011.559988.

83. *Ensuring Secure Seas: Indian Maritime Security Strategy*, Indian Navy, October 2015, https://www.indiannavy.nic.in/sites/default/files/Indian_Maritime_Security_Strategy_Document_25Jan16.pdf.

84. Amitendu Palit, "India's Act East policy and implications for Southeast Asia," *Southeast Asian Affairs* 2016: 81–92, https://www.jstor.org/stable/26466920?seq=1. For an overview of the Act East policy and the Indo-Pacific, see Dhruva Jaishankar, "Acting East: India in the Indo-Pacific," Brookings India, October 2019, https://www.brookings.edu/wp-content/uploads/2019/10/Acting-East-India-in-the-INDO-PACIFIC-without-cutmark.pdf.

85. Darshana M. Baruah, "Strengthening Delhi's strategic partnerships in the Indian Ocean," Center for New American Security, October 23, 2019, https://www.cnas.org/publications/reports/strengthening-delhis-strategic-partnerships-in-the-indianocean.

86. Darshana M. Baruah, "Islands of opportunity: Where India and Australia can work together," *The Interpreter*, Lowy Institute, May 22, 2020, https://www.lowyinstitute.org/the-interpreter/islands-opportunity-where-india-and-australia-can-work-together.

87. Darshana M. Baruah, "India in the Indo-Pacific: New Delhi's theater of opportunity," Carnegie Endowment for International Peace, June 30, 2020, https://carnegieindia.org/2020/06/30/india-in-indo-pacific-new-delhi-s-theater-of-opportunity-pub-82205.

88. Ashley J. Tellis, "Hustling in the Himalayas: The Sino-Indian border confrontation," Carnegie Endowment for International Peace, June 4, 2020, https://carnegieendowment.org/2020/06/04/hustling-in-himalayas-sino-indian-border-confrontation-pub-81979.

89. C. Raja Mohan, "Indian resistance to China's expansionism would be a definitive moment in Asia's geopolitical evolution," *The Indian Express*, June 30, 2020, https://indianexpress.com/article/opinion/columns/galwan-encounter-india-china-border-dispute-russia-us-india-foreign-relations-c-rajamohan-6482305/.

90. Rajat Pandit, "LAC face-off: Ladakh triggers Andamans build-up," *The Times of India*, July 4, 2020, https://timesofindia.indiatimes.com/india/ladakh-triggers-andamans-build-up/articleshow/76778355.cms; Admiral Arun Prakash, "Why isn't India using its 'maritime leverage' against China," *The Quint*, July 1, 2020, https://www.thequint.com/voices/opinion/india-china-navy-maritime-strategy-conflict-indian-ocean-south-china-sea-trade-choke-points.

91. Ian Storey, "China's Malacca dilemma," *China Brief* 6, no. 8 (The Jamestown Foundation, April 12, 2006), https://jamestown.org/program/chinas-malacca-dilemma/.

92. Vijay Gokhale, "There is a pressing need for India to develop a comprehensive Underwater Domain Awareness strategy," *The Indian Express*, June 23, 2020, https://indianexpress.com/article/opinion/columns/india-china-border-dispute-galwan-sea-route-6471403/.

93. H.I. Sutton, "China deployed 12 underwater drones in the Indian Ocean," *Forbes*, March 22, 2020, https://www.forbes.com/sites/hisutton/2020/03/22/china-deployed-underwater-drones-in-indian-ocean/#75c4969c6693.

94. Gokhale, "There is a pressing need for India to develop a comprehensive Underwater Domain Awareness Strategy."

95. The Malacca Strait is a busy commercial route. International law and traffic density (to avoid accidents) dictates that all sub-surface vessels must surface while transiting the straits. As a result, the Indian and US navies believe China to be using alternate routes, which are non-navigable for commercial vessels.

96. Desmond Ball and Richard Tanter, *The Tools of Owatatsumi: Japan's Ocean Surveillance and Coastal Defence Capabilities*, (Canberra: Australian National University Press, 2015), https://press.anu.edu.au/publications/tools-owatatsumi.

6 Shaping the Next Decades of the Indian Ocean

1. Senior Colonel Zhou Bo, International Maritime Security Conference, May 2023, https://www.rsis.edu.sg/research/idss/research-programmes/maritime-security-programme/imsc/.

2. C. Uday Bhaskar, "The Indian Navy—challenges of a Cinderella service," *Canadian Nautical Research Service*, October 18, 2017, https://www.cnrs-scrn.org/northern_mariner/vol24/tnm_24_34_75-81.pdf; Iskander Rehman, "India's aspirational naval doctrine," Carnegie Endowment for International Peace, October 15, 2012, https://carnegieendowment.org/2012/10/15/india-s-aspirational-naval-doctrine-pub-49694.
3. "What's behind the India–China border stand-off?," *BBC News*, July 5, 2017, https://www.bbc.com/news/world-asia-40478813.
4. Sameer P. Lalwani, Daniel Markey, and Vikram J. Singh, "Another clash on the India–China border underscores risks of militarization," United States Institute of Peace, December 20, 2022, https://www.usip.org/publications/2022/12/another-clash-india-china-border-underscores-risks-militarization.
5. Baruah, "India in the Indo-Pacific: New Delhi's theater of opportunity."
6. Kevin Bilms, "The Cod Wars and lessons for maritime counterinsurgency," US Naval Institute, February, 2023, https://www.usni.org/magazines/proceedings/2023/february/cod-wars-and-lessons-maritime-counterinsurgency.
7. Steven Lee Myers, Agnes Chang, Derek Watkins, and Claire Fu, "How China targets the global fish supply," *The New York Times*, September 26, 2022, https://www.nytimes.com/interactive/2022/09/26/world/asia/china-fishing-south-america.html; Ed Ou, Will N. Miller, and Ian Urbina, "'Squid fleet' takes you into the opaque world of Chinese fishing," *The New Yorker*, October 11, 2023, https://www.newyorker.com/culture/the-new-yorker-documentary/squid-fleet-takes-you-into-the-opaque-world-of-chinese-fishing; Terence McGinley, "A clear look at China's deep-sea fishing," *The New York Times*, October 9, 2022, https://www.nytimes.com/2022/10/09/insider/a-clear-look-at-chinas-deep-sea-fishing.html.
8. Kelley M. Sayler, "Climate change and adaptation: Department of Defense," Congressional Research Service, April 6, 2023, https://crsreports.congress.gov/product/pdf/IF/IF12161.
9. Darshana M. Baruah, "India's answer to the Belt and Road: A road map for South Asia," Carnegie Endowment for International Peace, August, 21, 2018, https://carnegieindia.org/2018/08/21/india-s-answer-to-belt-and-road-road-map-for-south-asia-pub-77071.
10. Nicholas Szechenyi, ed., *China's Maritime Silk Road: Strategic and Economic Implications for the Indo-Pacific Region*, Washington, DC: Center for Strategic and International Studies, March 2018.
11. S. Jaishankar, Speech by India's foreign secretary at Raisina Dialogue in New Delhi, Ministry of External Affairs, March 2, 2016, https://www.mea.gov.in/Speeches-Statements.htm?dtl/26433.
12. C. Raja Mohan, "Raja Mandala: Battle for islands", *The Indian Express*, November 20, 2018, https://indianexpress.com/article/opinion/columns/china-sri-lanka-pacific-islands-navy-strategic-united-states-maldives-mahinda-rajpaksa-raja-mandala-battle-for-islands-5454469/; Geoffrey Till, "The growing strategic significance of islands," *RSIS Commentary*, November 4, 2019, https://www.rsis.edu.sg/rsis-publication/rsis/the-growing-strategic-significance-of-islands/.
13. Baruah, "India's answer to the Belt and Road."

14. "China's nuclear submarines in Gulf of Aden could cause unease: Experts", *The Economic Times,* April 28, 2015, https://economictimes.indiatimes.com/news/defence/chinas-nuclear-submarines-in-gulf-of-aden-could-cause-unease-experts/articleshow/47083578.cms?from=mdr.

15. *Achieving Blue Growth: Building Vibrant Fisheries and Aquaculture Communities,* Food and Agriculture Organization of the United Nations, 2018, http://www.fao.org/3/CA0268EN/ca0268en.pdf.

16. Ibid.

17. Economic Development Board Mauritius, Deep Ocean Water Application (DOWA), https://edbmauritius.org/sector/deep-sea-application.

18. Economic Development Board Mauritius, "Blue economy", https://edbmauritius.org/blue-economy.

19. John Roach, "Under the sea, Microsoft tests a datacenter that's quick to deploy, could provide internet connectivity for years," *Microsoft,* June 5, 2018, https://news.microsoft.com/features/under-the-sea-microsoft-tests-a-datacenter-thats-quick-to-deploy-could-provide-internet-connectivity-for-years/.

Bibliography

Books

Amrith, Sunil, *Unruly Waters: How Rains, Rivers, Coasts, and Seas Have Shaped Asia's History* (New York: Hachette, 2018).

Anderson, Clare, Madhumita Mazumdar, and Vichvajit Pandya, *New Histories of the Andaman Islands: Landscape, Place and Identity in the Bay of Bengal, 1790–2012* (Cambridge: Cambridge University Press, 2016).

Asada, Sadao, *From Mahan to Pearl Harbor: The Imperial Japanese Navy and the United States* (Annapolis, MD: Naval Institute Press, 2006).

Ball, Desmond and Richard Tanter, *The Tools of Owatatsumi: Japan's Ocean Surveillance and Coastal Defence Capabilities* (Canberra: Australian National University Press, 2015).

Basrur, Rajesh, Anit Mukherjee, and T.V. Paul, *India-China Maritime Competition: The Security Dilemma at Sea* (London: Routledge, 2019).

Bose, Sugata, *A Hundred Horizons: The Indian Ocean in the Age of Global Empire* (Cambridge, MA and London: Harvard University Press, 2006).

Brewster, David, *India's Ocean: The Story of India's Bid for Regional Leadership* (Abingdon and New York: Routledge, 2014).

Calder, Kent E., *Embattled Garrisons: Comparative Base Politics and American Globalism* (Princeton, NJ: Princeton University Press, 2008).

Crowley, Roger, *Conquerors: How Portugal Seized the Indian Ocean and Forged the First Global Empire* (London: Faber & Faber, 2015).

Dingwall, Joanna, *International Law and Corporate Actors in Deep Seabed Mining* (Oxford: Oxford University Press, 2021).

Gordon, John Steele, *A Thread Across the Ocean: The Heroic Story of the Transatlantic Cable* (New York: Walker & Co., 2002).

Hiranandani, Vice Admiral Gulab Mohanlal, *Transition to Triumph: History of the Indian Navy, 1965–1975* (New Delhi: Lance Publishers, 2000).

Hu Bo, *Chinese Maritime Power in the 21st Century: Strategic Planning, Policy and Predictions* (London: Routledge, 2020).

Jackson, Ashley, *Of Islands, Ports and Sea Lanes: Africa and the Indian Ocean in the Second World War* (Warwick: Helion, 2018).

Jackson, Ashley, *War and Empire in Mauritius and the Indian Ocean* (London: Palgrave Macmillan, 2001).

Kaplan, Robert D., *Monsoon: The Indian Ocean and the Future of American Power* (New York: Random House, 2010).

Kaplan, Robert D., *The Revenge of Geography: What the Map Tells Us about Coming Conflicts and the Battle against Fate* (New York: Random House, 2012).

Kaul, Sanat, *Andaman and Nicobar Islands: India's Untapped Strategic Assets* (New Delhi: Pentagon Press, 2015).

Kulke, Hermann, K. Kesavapany, and Vijay Sakhuja, eds, *Nagapattinam to Suvarnadwipa: Reflections on the Chola Naval Expeditions to Southeast Asia* (Singapore: Institute of Southeast Asian Studies, 2009).

Lambert, Andrew D., *Seapower States: Maritime Culture, Continental Empires, and the Conflict That Made the Modern World* (New Haven, CT and London: Yale University Press, 2018).

Lintner, Bertil, *The Costliest Pearl: China's Struggle for India's Ocean* (London: Hurst, 2019).

Mahan, Alfred T., *Mahan on Naval Strategy: Selections from the Writings of Rear Admiral Alfred Thayer Mahan* (Annapolis: Naval Institute Press, 2015).

Menon, Shivshankar, *India and Asian Geopolitics: The Past, Present* (Washington, DC: Brookings Institution Press, 2021).

Miller, Edward S., *War Plan Orange: The US Strategy to Defeat Japan, 1897–1945* (Annapolis, MD: Naval Institute Press, 1991).

Misra, Raj Narain, *Indian Ocean and India's Security* (New Delhi: Mittal Publication, 1986).

Mohan, C. Raja, *Samudra Manthan: Sino-Indian Rivalry in the Indo-Pacific* (Washington, DC: Carnegie Endowment for International Peace, 2012).

Morison, Samuel E., *The Two-Ocean War: A Short History of the United States Navy in the Second World War* (Boston, MA: Little, Brown, 1963).

Murthy, R.V.R., *Andaman and Nicobar Islands: Development and Decentralization* (New Delhi: Mittal Publications, 2005).

Pande, Aparna, *From Chanakya to Modi: Evolution of India's Foreign Policy* (New Delhi: HarperCollins, 2017).

Panikkar, K.M., *India and the Indian Ocean* (London: George Allen & Unwin, 1945).

Pauli, Gunter, *The Blue Economy: 10 Years, 100 Innovations, 100 Million Jobs* (Taos, NM: Paradigm Publications, 2010).

Pearson, Michael N., *The Indian Ocean* (London: Routledge, 2003).

Polo, Marco, *The Travels of Marco Polo: The Complete Yule-Cordier Edition*, 2 vols. (New York: Dover Publications, 1920).

Raghavan, Srinath, *1971: A Global History of the Creation of Bangladesh* (Cambridge, MA: Harvard University Press, 2013).

Remmelink, Willem (trans.), *Second Senshi Sosho Volume: The Operations of the Navy in the Dutch East Indies and the Bay of Bengal*, War History Office of the National Defense College of Japan (Leiden: Leiden University Press, 2018).

Schnepel, Burkhard, *Small Island, Large Ocean: Mauritius and the Indian Ocean World* (Abingdon: Routledge, 2023).

Singh, Rear Admiral Satyindra, *Blueprint to Bluewater: The Indian Navy 1951–65* (New Delhi: Lance Publishers, 1992).

Starosielski, Nicole, *The Undersea Network* (Durham, NC: Duke University Press, 2015).

Stavridis, Adm. James, *Sea Power: The History and Geopolitics of the World's Oceans* (New York: Penguin Random House, 2017).

Vaidik, Aparna, *Imperial Andamans: Colonial Encounter and Island History* (London: Palgrave Macmillan, 2010).

Vine, David, *Island of Shame: The Secret History of the US Military Base on Diego Garcia* (Princeton, NJ: Princeton University Press, 2009).

Articles and reports

Abe, H.E. Mr. Shinzo, "Speech to the Parliament of the Republic of India: Confluence of the Two Seas," Ministry of Foreign Affairs of Japan, August 22, 2007, https://www.mofa.go.jp/region/asia-paci/pmv0708/speech-2.html.

Abi-Habib, Maria, "How China got Sri Lanka to cough up a port," *The New York Times*, June 25, 2018, https://www.nytimes.com/2018/06/25/world/asia/china-sri-lanka-port.html.

Achieving Blue Growth: Building Vibrant Fisheries and Aquaculture Communities, Food and Agriculture Organization of the United Nations, http://www.fao.org/3/CA0268EN/ca0268en.pdf.

"AIS (Automatic Identification System) overview," NATO Shipping Center, https://shipping.nato.int/nsc/operations/news/2021/ais-automatic-identification-system-overview.

"Ambassador of Union of Comoros to China: Mining Town Inspires Young People in Comoros," *People's Daily Overseas Edition*, August 9, 2022, https://eng.yidai-yilu.gov.cn/p/267461.html.

Anandakuan, Nithyani, "The Sri Lankan civil war and its history, revisited in 2020," *Harvard International Review*, August 31, 2020, https://hir.harvard.edu/sri-lankan-civil-war/.

"Andaman & Nicobar can be springboard for India's Look East policy," *The Economic Times*, January 11, 2014, https://economictimes.indiatimes.com/news/politics-and-nation/andaman-nicobar-can-be-springboard-for-indias-look-east-policy-pranab-mukherjee/articleshow/28686775.cms?from=mdr.

Andaman and Nicobar Islands, Ministry of Tribal Affairs, https://tribal.nic.in/notificationAndaman.aspx.

"Andamans: US man's death puts spotlight on tribal tourism," *BBC News*, November 23, 2018, https://www.bbc.com/news/world-asia-india-46313965.

Anthropological Survey of India, Ministry of Culture, Government of India, https://ansi.gov.in/regional-centre-andaman-niccobar/.

Arora, Rajat, "Modi government's 10,000 crore plan to transform Andaman and Nicobar islands," *The Economic Times*, June 26, 2015, https://economictimes.indiatimes.com/news/economy/infrastructure/modi-governments-rs-10000-crore-plan-to-transform-andaman-and-nicobar-islands/articleshow/49111067.cms.

Ayers, Alyssa, "The US Indo-Pacific Strategy Needs More Indian Ocean," Council on Foreign Relations, January 22, 2019, http://www.cfr.org/expert-brief/us-indo-pacific-strategy-needs-more-indian-ocean.

Ayers, Alyssa, "Will India Start Acting Like a Global Power? New Delhi's Role New Role," *Foreign Affairs*, October 16, 2017, http://foreignaffairs.com/articles/india/2017-10-16/will-india-start-acting-global-power.

Baruah, Darshana M., "India in the Indo-Pacific: New Delhi's theater of opportunity," Carnegie Endowment for International Peace, June 30, 2020, https://carnegieendowment.org/2020/06/30/india-in-indo-pacific-new-delhi-s-theater-of-opportunity-pub-82205.

Baruah, Darshana M., "India's answer to the Belt and Road: A road map for South Asia," Carnegie Endowment for International Peace, August, 21, 2018, https://carnegieindia.org/2018/08/21/india-s-answer-to-belt-and-road-road-map-for-south-asia-pub-77071.

Baruah, Darshana M., "Islands of opportunity: Where India and Australia can work together," *The Interpreter*, Lowy Institute, May 22, 2020, https://www.lowyinstitute.org/the-interpreter/islands-opportunity-where-india-and-australia-can-work-together.

Baruah, Darshana M., "Showing up is half the battle: US maritime forces in the Indian Ocean," *War on the Rocks,* March 18, 2021, https://warontherocks.com/2021/03/showing-up-is-half-the-battle-u-s-maritime-forces-in-the-indian-ocean/.

Baruah, Darshana M., "Sister islands in the Indian Ocean region: Linking the Andaman and Nicobar Islands to La Réunion," *War on the Rocks*, March 20, 2019, https://warontherocks.com/2019/03/sister-islands-in-the-indian-ocean-region-linking-the-andaman-and-nicobar-islands-to-la-reunion/.

Baruah, Darshana M., "Strengthening Delhi's strategic partnerships in the Indian Ocean," Center for New American Security, October 23, 2019, https://www.cnas.org/publications/reports/strengthening-delhis-strategic-partnerships-in-the-indianocean.

Baruah, Darshana M., "Testimony: Surrounding the ocean: PRC influence in the Indian Ocean," US House of Representatives Committee on Foreign Affairs, April 18, 2023, https://docs.house.gov/meetings/FA/FA05/20230418/115667/HHRG-118-FA05-Wstate-BaruahD-20230418.pdf.

Baruah, Darshana M., "The three things the United States must do at its historic Pacific Islands Summit," Carnegie Endowment for International Peace, September 28, 2022, https://carnegieendowment.org/2022/09/28/three-things-united-states-must-do-at-its-historic-pacific-islands-summit-pub-88033.

Baruah, Darshana M., "View: African islands in the Indian Ocean—Looking beyond Delhi's strategic blindness," *The Economic Times*, October 17, 2019, https://economictimes.indiatimes.com/news/defence/view-african-islands-in-the-indian-ocean-looking-beyond-delhis-strategic-blindness/articleshow/71627802.cms

Baruah, Darshana M., Nitya Labh, and Jessica Greely, *Mapping the Indian Ocean Region*, Report, Washington, DC: Carnegie Endowment for International Peace, June 2023, https://carnegieendowment.org/2023/06/15/mapping-indian-ocean-region-pub-89971.

Bashfield, Samuel, "Mauritian sovereignty over the Chagos Archipelago? Strategic implications for Diego Garcia from a UK–US perspective," *Journal of the Indian Ocean Region* 16 (2020): 166–181.

Basu, Nayanima, "Show gratitude to India, Mauritius PM tells oppn as Agalega Island row adds to snooping fire," *ThePrint*, July 29, 2022, https://theprint.in/diplomacy/show-gratitude-to-india-mauritius-pm-tells-oppn-as-agalega-island-row-adds-to-snooping-fire/1060764/.

Bergold, Harry A., Jr., "Memorandum from the Deputy Assistant Secretary of Defense for European and NATO Affairs (Bergold) to the Deputy Assistant Secretary of Defense for Security Assistance (Peet)," US Department of State: Office of the Historian, Washington, January 17, 1974, https://history.state.gov/historicaldocuments/frus1969-76ve08/d65.

Bezboruah, Monoranjan, *US Strategy in the Indian Ocean: The International Response* (Westport, CT: Praeger, 1977).

Bhaskar, C. Uday, "The Indian Navy—challenges of a Cinderella service," *Canadian Nautical Research Service*, October 18, 2017, https://www.cnrs-scrn.org/northern_mariner/vol24/tnm_24_34_75-81.pdf.

Bhattacherjee, Kallol, "Kissinger, Nixon 'helped' Pakistan in 1971, documents from US archive reveal," *The Hindu*, December 1, 2023, https://www.thehindu.com/news/national/kissinger-nixon-broke-us-rule-to-help-pakistan-sent-aircraft-from-third-countries-as-they-feared-india-was-about-to-attack-west-pakistan/article67591823.ece.

Bilms, Kevin, "The Cod Wars and lessons for maritime counterinsurgency," US Naval Institute, February 2023, https://www.usni.org/magazines/proceedings/2023/february/cod-wars-and-lessons-maritime-counterinsurgency.

Blanchy, Sophie, "A matrilineal and matrilocal Muslim society in flux: Negotiating gender and family relations in the Comoros," *Africa* 89, no.1 (February 2019): 21–39.

Bosack, Michael MacArthur, "Understanding Japan's southwest islands buildup," *The Japan Times*, April 22, 2019, https://www.japantimes.co.jp/opinion/2019/04/22/commentary/japan-commentary/understanding-japans-southwest-islands-buildup/.

Bradford, John F., "The maritime strategy of the United States: Implications for Indo-Pacific sea lanes." *Contemporary Southeast Asia* 33, no. 2 (2011): 183–208, http://www.jstor.org/stable/41288826. http://www.jstor.org/stable/41288826.

Brautigam, Deborah and Meg Rithmire, "The Chinese debt trap is a myth," *The Atlantic*, February 6, 2021, https://www.theatlantic.com/international/archive/2021/02/china-debt-trap-diplomacy/617953/.

Braw, Elisabeth, "Decoupling is already happening—under the sea," *Foreign Policy*, May 24, 2023, https://foreignpolicy.com/2023/05/24/china-subsea-cables-internet-decoupling-biden/.

Bruce, David K.E., "Telegram From the Embassy in the United Kingdom to the Department of State," US Department of State, London, September 4, 1968, 1037Z, https://history.state.gov/historicaldocuments/frus1964-68v21/d50.

Burdette, Lane, "Leveraging submarine cables for political gain: US responses to Chinese strategy," *Journal of Public & International Affairs* 32, no. 1 (May 2021), https://jpia.princeton.edu/news/leveraging-submarine-cables-political-gain-us-responses-chinese-strategy.

Centre for Coastal Zone Management and Coastal Shelter Belt, Ministry of Environment, Forests and Climate Change, Government of India, http://iomenvis.nic.in/index2.aspx?slid=60&sublinkid=25&langid=1&mid=1.

Chaudhury, Dipanjan Roy, "India, France explore 3rd country projects in Western Indian Ocean region," *The Economic Times*, October 24, 2019, https://economictimes.indiatimes.com/news/defence/india-france-explore-3rd-country-projects-in-western-indian-ocean-region/articleshow/71743985.cms?from=mdr.

"China: Executive summary," US Energy Information Administration, August 8, 2022, https://www.eia.gov/international/analysis/country/CHN.

"China's nuclear submarines in Gulf of Aden could cause unease: Experts," *The Economic Times*, April 28, 2015, https://economictimes.indiatimes.com/news/defence/chinas-nuclear-submarines-in-gulf-of-aden-could-cause-unease-experts/articleshow/47083578.cms?from=mdr.

Clark, Aaron, "Suez snarl seen halting $9.6 billion a day of ship traffic," *Bloomberg News*, March 25, 2021, https://www.bloomberg.com/news/articles/2021-03-25/suez-snarl-seen-halting-9-6-billion-a-day-worth-of-ship-traffic.

Clifford, Catherine, "The Metals Company announces a controversial timeline for deep sea mining that worsens the divide already bitter battle," *CNBC*, August 4, 2023, https://www.cnbc.com/2023/08/04/the-metals-company-puts-out-controversial-timeline-for-deep-sea-mining.html.

Cordner, Lee, "Rethinking maritime security in the Indian Ocean region," *Journal of the Indian Ocean Region* 6, no. 1 (2010): 67–85.

Das, Pushpita, "Securing the Andaman and Nicobar Islands," *Journal of Strategic Analysis* 35 (2011), https://www.tandfonline.com/doi/full/10.1080/09700161.2011.559988.

DeSilva-Ranasinghe, Sergei, "Why the Indian Ocean matters," *The Diplomat*, March 2, 2011, https://thediplomat.com/2011/03/why-the-indian-ocean-matters/.

Economic Development Board Mauritius, Deep Ocean Water Application (DOWA), https://edbmauritius.org/sector/deep-sea-application.

"Editorial note," US Department of State: Office of the Historian, Washington, October 3, 1970, https://history.state.gov/historicaldocuments/frus1969-76v24/d41.

"Editorial note," US Department of State: Office of the Historian, Washington, November 25, 1970, https://history.state.gov/historicaldocuments/frus1969-76v24/d44.

Ensuring Secure Seas: Indian Maritime Security Strategy, Indian Navy, October 2015, https://www.indiannavy.nic.in/sites/default/files/Indian_Maritime_Security_Strategy_Document_25Jan16.pdf.

From Surprise to Reckoning: The Kargil Review Committee Report (New Delhi: Sage Publications, December 15, 1999).

Gladstone, Rick and Megan Specia, "What to know about the Suez Canal and the cargo ship that was stuck there," *The New York Times*, updated January 1, 2022, https://www.nytimes.com/2021/03/25/world/middleeast/suez-canal-container-ship.html.

Gokhale, Vijay, "There is a pressing need for India to develop a comprehensive Underwater Domain Awareness Strategy," *The Indian Express*, June 23, 2020, https://indianexpress.com/article/opinion/columns/india-china-border-dispute-galwan-sea-route-6471403/.

Goodman, Matthew P. and Matthew Wayland, "Securing Asia's subsea network: US interests and strategic options," Center for Strategic and International Studies, April 2022, https://www.csis.org/analysis/securing-asias-subsea-network-us-interests-and-strategic-options.

Government of Japan, "Defense of Japan 2023", Ministry of Defense, 2023, http://www.mod.go.jp/en/pub/w_paper/wp_2019.html.

Green, Michael J., *China's Maritime Silk Road: Strategic and Economic Implications for the Indo-Pacific Region*, Washington, DC: Center for Strategic and International Studies, April 2, 2018, https://www.csis.org/analysis/chinas-maritime-silk-road-strategic-and-economic-implications-indo-pacific-region.

Halperin, Morton H., *The 1958 Taiwan Straits Crisis: A Documented History* (Santa Monica, CA: RAND Corporation, 1966), https://www.rand.org/pubs/research_memoranda/RM4900.html.

Hameiri, Shahar, "Debunking the myth of China's debt trap diplomacy," *The Interpreter*, September 9, 2020, https://www.lowyinstitute.org/the-interpreter/debunking-myth-china-s-debt-trap-diplomacy.

"Incredible islands of India (holistic development)," NITI Aayog, https://niti.gov.in/writereaddata/files/document_publication/IslandsDev.pdf.

India State of Forest Report 2017, https://fsi.nic.in/isfr2017/andaman-nocobar-island-isfr-2017.pdf.

"The Indian Ocean Strategic Map, Regional Trade," Indian Ocean Initiative, Carnegie Endowment for International Peace, 2023, https://carnegieendowment.org/publications/interactive/indian-ocean-map/?page=Economy.

Indian Ocean Tuna Commission, Food and Agriculture Organization of the United Nations, *Status summary for species of Tuna and Tuna-like species under the IOTC Fisheries*, 2021, https://www.fao.org/fishery/en/collection/iotc_ssr.

Jaishankar, Dhruva, "Acting East: India in the Indo-Pacific," Brookings India, October 2019, https://www.brookings.edu/wp-content/uploads/2019/10/Acting-East-India-in-the-INDO-PACIFIC-without-cutmark.pdf.

Jaishankar, S., speech by India's foreign secretary at Raisina Dialogue in New Delhi, Ministry of External Affairs, March 2, 2016, https://www.mea.gov.in/Speeches-Statements.htm?dtl/26433.

Joint Chiefs of Staff, "Memorandum for the Secretary of Defense, subject: Indian Ocean islands," US Department of State: Office of the Historian, Washington, May 20, 1965.

Joint Chiefs of Staff, "Memorandum from the Joint Chiefs of Staff to Secretary of Defense McNamara," US Department of State: Office of the Historian, Washington, July 25, 1967, https://history.state.gov/historicaldocuments/frus-964-68v21/d45.

Joint Chiefs of Staff, "Memorandum from the Joint Chiefs of Staff to Secretary of Defense McNamara," US Department of State: Office of the Historian, Washington, April 10, 1968, https://history.state.gov/historicaldocuments/frus-964-68v21/d47.

Jones, Lee and Shahar Hameiri, "Debunking the myth of debt-trap diplomacy," Chatham House, August 19, 2020, https://www.chathamhouse.org/2020/08/debunking-myth-debt-trap-diplomacy.

Joshi, Yogesh, "Sailing through the Cold War: Indian Navy quest for a submarine arm, 1947–67," *India Review* 17, no. 5 (2018), 476–504.

Kardon, Isaac and Sarah Camacho, "Why China, not the United States, is making the rules for deep-sea mining," Carnegie Endowment for International Peace, December 19, 2023, https://carnegieendowment.org/2023/12/19/why-china-not-united-states-is-making-rules-for-deep-sea-mining-pub-91298.

Kargil Committee Report: An Appraisal, https://archive.claws.in/images/journals_doc/1400824637Report%20of%20the%20Kargil%20Review%20Committee%20%20CJ%20SSummer%202009.pdf.

Kissinger, Henry, "National Security Study Memorandum 199: Indian Ocean Strategy," National Security Council of the USA, Washington, March 14, 1974, https://www.nixonlibrary.gov/sites/default/files/virtuallibrary/documents/nssm/nssm_199.pdf.

Koda, Yoji, "Island defense and seizure operations, and naval strategic lessons learned by Imperial Japan in the Pacific theater of operations during World War II," International Forum on War History, September 25, 2013, http://www.nids.mod.go.jp/english/event/forum/pdf/2013/02.pdf.

Koehring, Martin, "How to shift the ocean narrative for a sustainable blue economy," *Economist Impact,* October 27, 2022, https://impact.economist.com/ocean/sustainable-ocean-economy/how-to-shift-the-ocean-narrative-for-a-sustainable-blue-economy.

Komer, Robert, "Memorandum from the President's Deputy Special Assistant for National Security Affairs (Komer) to the President's Special Assistant for National Security Affairs (Bundy) and Francis Bator of the National Security Council Staff," US Department of State: Office of the Historian, Washington, January 26, 1966, https://history.state.gov/historicaldocuments/frus1964-68v21/d41.

Koonjul, Amb. Jagdish, speech at Ocean Nations: An Indo-Pacific Islands Dialogue, September 19–20, 2021, New York, https://carnegieendowment.org/2021/09/20/ocean-nations-indo-pacific-islands-dialogue-event-7680

Kumar, Sunaina and Angela Stanzel, "The Maldives crisis and the China–India chess match," *The Diplomat,* March 15, 2018, https://thediplomat.com/2018/03/the-maldives-crisis-and-the-china-india-chess-match/.

Lalwani, Sameer P., Daniel Markey, and Vikram J. Singh, "Another clash on the India–China border underscores risks of militarization," United States Institute of Peace, December 20, 2022, https://www.usip.org/publications/2022/12/another-clash-india-china-border-underscores-risks-militarization.

Lavani, Lt. Said, Regional Maritime Information Fusion Center, November 11, 2022, https://dcoc.org/wp-content/uploads/LAVAN-COMOROS-Presentation-of-RMIFC.pdf.

Lee, Ki-Hoon, Junsung Noh, and Jong Seong Khim, "The blue economy and the United Nations' sustainable development goals: Challenges and opportunities," *Environmental International* 137 (April 2020), https://doi.org/10.1016/j.envint.2020.105528.

Lu, Christina, "The country with nothing left to lose," *Foreign Policy,* February 11, 2024, https://foreignpolicy.com/2024/02/11/nauru-deep-sea-mining-economy-china-taiwan/.

Lu, Wenhai, et al., "Successful blue economy examples with an emphasis on international perspectives," *Frontiers in Marine Science* 6 (2019), https://doi.org/10.3389/fmars.2019.00261.

McBride, James, Noah Berman, and Andrew Chatzky, "China's massive Belt and Road Initiative," Council on Foreign Relations, February 2, 2023, https://www.cfr.org/backgrounder/chinas-massive-belt-and-road-initiative.

McGinley, Terence, "A clear look at China's deep-sea fishing," *The New York Times*, October 9, 2022, https://www.nytimes.com/2022/10/09/insider/a-clear-look-at-chinas-deep-sea-fishing.html.

McNamara, Robert S., "Memorandum from Secretary of Defense McNamara to the Secretary of the Navy (Ignatius)," US Department of State: Office of the Historian, Washington, October 27, 1967, https://history.state.gov/historicaldocuments/frus1964-68v21/d46.

Madan, Tanvi, "The Rise, Fall, and Rebirth of the Quad," *War on the Rocks*, November 16, 2019, http://warontherocks.com/2017/11/rise-fall-rebirth-quad/.

Madan, Tanvi, "The US, India, and the Indo-Pacific," *Seminar*, Vol. 715, March 1, 2019, http://www.india-seminar.com/2019/715/715_tanvi_madan.htm.

Manning, Robert A. and Bharath Gopalaswamy, "Is Abdulla Yameen handing over the Maldives to China?," *Foreign Policy*, March 21, 2018, https://foreignpolicy.com/2018/03/21/is-abdulla-yameen-handing-over-the-maldives-to-china/.

"Map: The strategic importance of the Indian Ocean," Carnegie Endowment for International Peace, September 2022, https://carnegieendowment.org/publications/interactive/indian-ocean-map/?page=Application---The-Strategic-Importance-of-the-Indian-Ocean.

"Mapping oil and gas contracts in the northern Mozambique Channel," World Wildlife Fund, https://wwf-sight.org/mapping-oil-and-gas-concessions-in-northern-mozambique-channel/.

Marlow, Jeffrey, "Undersea internet cables can detect earthquakes—and may soon warn of tsunamis," *The New Yorker*, July 26, 2022, https://www.newyorker.com/science/elements/undersea-internet-cables-can-detect-earthquakes-and-may-soon-warn-of-tsunamis.

"Mayotte votes for full French integration," *France24*, March 29, 2009, https://www.france24.com/en/20090329-mayotte-votes-full-french-integration-.

Medcalf, Rory, "The Indo-Pacific: What's in a name?" *The American Interest* 9, no. 2 (October 2013), https://www.the-american-interest.com/2013/10/10/the-indo-pacific-whats-in-a-ame/.

Menini, Elisabetta, Anindita Chakraborty, and Stephen E. Roady, "Public participation in seabed mining in areas beyond national jurisdiction: Lessons learned from national regulators in the terrestrial mining sector," *Marine Policy* 146 (December 2022), https://www.sciencedirect.com/science/article/pii/S0308597X22003554?via%3Dihub.

Meredith, Sam, "Trouble in paradise: All you need to know about the Maldives' ongoing political crisis," *CNBC*, February 8, 2018, https://www.cnbc.com/2018/02/08/maldives-crisis-all-you-need-to-know-about-the-political-turmoil.html.

Mohan, C. Raja, "Indian resistance to China's expansionism would be a definitive moment in Asia's geopolitical evolution," *The Indian Express*, June 30, 2020, https://indianexpress.com/article/opinion/columns/galwan-encounter-india-china-border-dispute-russia-us-india-foreign-relations-c-rajamohan-6482305/.

Mohan, C. Raja, "Raja Mandala: Battle for islands", *The Indian Express*, November 20, 2018, https://indianexpress.com/article/opinion/columns/china-sri-lanka-pacific-islands-navy-strategic-united-states-maldives-mahinda-rajpaksa-raja-mandala-battle-for-islands-5454469/.

Mohan, C. Raja and Darshana M. Baruah, "Deepening the India–France maritime partnership," Carnegie Endowment for International Peace, February 26, 2018, https://carnegieendowment.org/files/Mohan_Baruah_Deepening_The_India_France_Maritime_Partnership.pdf.

Mohan, Garima, "Great Game in the Indian Ocean," Global Public Policy Institute, June 11, 2018, http://gppi.net/2018/06/11/great-game-in-the-indian-ocean.

Moorer, Thomas Hinman, "Paper Prepared in the Office of the Chief of Naval Operations (Moorer)," US Department of State: Office of the Historian, Washington, February 11, 1970, https://history.state.gov/historicaldocuments/frus1969-76v24/d39.

Mouat, Frederic John, "Narrative of an expedition to the Andaman Islands in 1857," *Journal of the Royal Geographical Society of London*, 32 (London, 1862), 109–126.

Mukherjee, Anit, "India's Joint Andaman and Nicobar Command is a failed experiment," *Asia Pacific Bulletin, East-West Center*, November 17, 2015, https://www.eastwestcenter.org/system/tdf/private/apb289.pdf?file=1&type=node&id=34843

Muralidharan, Vice Admiral M.P., "Economic and strategic importance of sea in modern Indian context," *Indian Defense Review*, February 28, 2019, http://www.indiandefencereview.com/spotlights/economic-and-strategic-importance-of-sea-in-modern-indian-context/.

Mullen, Rani D. and Cody Poplin, "The New Great Game: A Battle for Access and Influence in the Indo-Pacific," *Foreign Affairs*, September 29, 2015, http://foreignaffairs.com/articles/china/2015-09-29/new-great-game.

Myers, Steven Lee, Agnes Chang, Derek Watkins, and Claire Fu, "How China targets the global fish supply," *The New York Times*, September 26, 2022, https://www.nytimes.com/interactive/2022/09/26/world/asia/china-fishing-south-america.html.

Ngari, Allan and Clive Baldwin, "Let Chagossians go home, decide their future," Human Rights Watch, June 21, 2023, https://www.hrw.org/news/2023/06/21/let-chagossians-go-home-decide-their-future.

Nitze, Paul H., "Memorandum from the Deputy Secretary of Defense (Nitze)," US Department of State: Office of the Historian, Washington, June 15, 1968, https://history.state.gov/historicaldocuments/frus1964-68v21/d48.

Noor, Elina, "Entangled: Southeast Asia and the geopolitics of undersea cables," *University of Hawai'i at Manoa Center for Indo-Pacific Affairs Indo-Pacific Outlook* 1, no. 5 (February 7, 2024), https://manoa.hawaii.edu/indopacificaffairs/article/entangled-southeast-asia-and-the-geopolitics-of-undersea-cables/.

Office of the Secretary of Defense, *Annual Report to Congress: Military and Security Developments Involving the People's Republic of China*, US Department of Defense, https://media.defense.gov/2021/Nov/03/2002885874/-1/-1/0/2021-CMPR-FINAL.PDF.

Ou, Ed, Will N. Miller, and Ian Urbina, "'Squid fleet' takes you into the opaque world of Chinese fishing," *The New Yorker*, October 11, 2023, https://www.newyorker.com/culture/the-new-yorker-documentary/squid-fleet-takes-you-into-the-opaque-world-of-chinese-fishing.

BIBLIOGRAPHY

Pal, Deep, "China's influence in South Asia: Vulnerabilities and resilience in four countries," Carnegie Endowment for International Peace, October 13, 2021, https://carnegieendowment.org/2021/10/13/china-s-influence-in-south-asia-vulnerabilities-and-resilience-in-four-countries-pub-85552.

Palit, Amitendu, "India's Act East policy and implications for Southeast Asia," *Southeast Asian Affairs* (2016): 81–92, https://www.jstor.org/stable/26466920?seq=1.

Pandit, Rajat, "LAC face-off: Ladakh triggers Andaman's build-up," *The Times of India*, July 4, 2020, https://timesofindia.indiatimes.com/india/ladakh-triggers-andamans-build-up/articleshow/76778355.cms.

Patalano, Alessio, "Japan as a seapower: Strategy, doctrine, and capabilities under three defence reviews, 1995–2010," *Journal of Strategic Studies* 37 (2014), https://www.tandfonline.com/doi/abs/10.1080/01402390.2014.904788?src=recsys&journalCode=fjss20.

Peri, Dinakar, "Navy's new air base in north of Port Blair," *The Hindu*, January 7, 2019, https://www.thehindu.com/news/national/navys-new-air-base-in-north-of-port-blair/article25934644.ece.

Prakash, Arun, "Evolution of the Indian Navy: Towards a 'maritime awakening'?", in Harsh V. Pant, ed., *The Routledge Handbook of Indian Defence Policy: Themes, Structures and Doctrines* (New Delhi: Routledge, 2020).

Prakash, Admiral Arun, "Why isn't India using its 'maritime leverage' against China," *The Quint*, July 1, 2020, https://www.thequint.com/voices/opinion/india-china-navy-maritime-strategy-conflict-indian-ocean-south-china-sea-trade-choke-points.

Prasad, Satyendra and Emily Hardy, "Why Pacific island states are concerned about deep-sea mining," Carnegie Endowment for International Peace, November 27, 2023, https://carnegieendowment.org/2023/11/27/why-pacific-island-states-are-concerned-about-deep-sea-mining-pub-91051.

"Prime Minister's speech at the East Asia Summit," Ministry of External Affairs, Government of India, November 4, 2019, https://www.mea.gov.in/Speeches-Statements.htm?dtl/32171/Prime_Ministers_Speech_at_the_East_Asia_Summit_04_November_2019.

Qayum, Nayma, "The crisis in the Maldives, explained," *The Washington Post*, February 12, 2018, https://www.washingtonpost.com/news/monkey-cage/wp/2018/02/12/how-is-trade-with-china-related-to-the-state-of-emergency-in-maldives-heres-what-you-need-to-know/.

Rana, Himanil, "Missing in action: India's aircraft carriers," *The Interpreter*, Lowy Institute, October 11, 2018, https://www.lowyinstitute.org/the-interpreter/missing-action-india-aircraft-carriers.

Rehman, Iskander, "India's aspirational naval doctrine," Carnegie Endowment for International Peace, October 15, 2012, https://carnegieendowment.org/2012/10/15/india-s-aspirational-naval-doctrine-pub-49694.

Ritzen, Yarno "Evidence points to secret Indian Navy base on Mauritian island," *Al-Jazeera*, August 3, 2021, https://www.aljazeera.com/news/2021/8/3/evidence-points-to-secret-indian-navy-base-on-mauritian-island.

Roach, John, "Under the sea, Microsoft tests a datacenter that's quick to deploy, could provide internet connectivity for years," *Microsoft*, June 5, 2018, https://news.microsoft.com/features/under-the-sea-microsoft-tests-a-datacenter-thats-quick-to-deploy-could-provide-internet-connectivity-for-years/.

Rusk, Dean, "Telegram from the Department of State to the Embassy in the United Kingdom," US Department of State: Office of the Historian, Washington, July 3, 1968, 1912Z, https://history.state.gov/historicaldocuments/frus1964-68v21/d49.

Sayler, Kelley M., "Climate change and adaptation: Department of Defense," Congressional Research Service, April 6, 2023, https://crsreports.congress.gov/product/pdf/IF/IF12161.

Scott, David, "Britain returns to the Indian Ocean," *Commonwealth Journal of International Affairs* 107 (2018): 307–316.

Sengupta, Sudipto, "Madhumala Chattopadhaya, the woman who made the Sentinelese put their arrows down," *The Print*, November 29, 2018, https://theprint.in/opinion/madhumala-chattopadhyay-the-woman-who-made-the-sentinelese-put-their-arrows-down/156330/.

Shahid, Abdulla, "Why small island states are vulnerable but not powerless," Carnegie Endowment for International Peace, September 27, 2022, https://carnegieendowment.org/2022/09/27/why-small-island-states-are-vulnerable-but-not-powerless-pub-88015.

Sherman, Justin, "Cyber defense across the ocean floor: The geopolitics of submarine cable security," Atlantic Council, September 13, 2021, https://www.atlanticcouncil.org/in-depth-research-reports/report/cyber-defense-across-the-ocean-floor-the-geopolitics-of-submarine-cable-security/.

"Shri Amit Shah chairs meeting of the Island Development Agency focusing on green development in the islands to reach a new height," Press Information Bureau, Ministry of Home Affairs, Government of India, January 13, 2020, https://pib.gov.in/Pressreleaseshare.aspx?PRID=1599301.

Simoes, A.J.G. and C.A. Hidalgo, "The Economic Complexity Observatory: An analytical tool for understanding the dynamics of economic development," 2011, https://oec.world/en/resources/about.

Singh, Abhijit. "Blue economy in the Indo-Pacific: Navigating between growth and conservation," Observer Research Fund, July 28, 2021, https://www.orfonline.org/research/blue-economy-in-the-indo-pacific/.

Smith-Godfrey, Simone, "Defining the blue economy," *Maritime Affairs Journal of the National Maritime Foundation of India* 12, no. 1 (April 2016): 58–64, https://doi.org/10.1080/09733159.2016.1175131.

Snyder, Michael, "Kanhoji Angre: India's first naval commander," Gateway House, September 4, 2012, https://www.gatewayhouse.in/kanhoji-angre-indias-first-naval-commander/

Sood, Jyotika and Utpal Bhaskar, "Eye on China, India plans infrastructure boost in Andaman and Nicobar islands," *LiveMint*, June 26, 2017, https://www.livemint.com/Politics/TDQmSWIJKb8CazbITu0tCN/Eye-on-China-India-plans-infrastructure-boost-in-Andaman-an.html.

"Sri Lanka China relations," Embassy of the Democratic Socialist Republic of Sri Lanka, https://www.beijing.embassy.gov.lk/srirelation.

"State Action Plan on Climate Change," Ministry of Environment, Forest, and Climate Change, November, 2013, http://moef.gov.in/wp-content/uploads/2017/08/Andaman-and-Nicobar.pdf.

Storey, Ian, "China's Malacca dilemma," *China Brief* 6, no. 8 (The Jamestown Foundation, April 12, 2006), https://jamestown.org/program/chinas-malacca-dilemma/.

"The Strait of Hormuz is the world's most important oil transit chokepoint," US Energy Information Administration, June 20, 2019.

"Study Prepared in Response to National Security Study Memorandum 199: US IOR Strategy 1976," US Department of State: Office of the Historian, Washington, undated, https://history.state.gov/historicaldocuments/frus1969-76ve08/d77.

Sullivan de Estrada, Kate, "India and the Quad: When a Weak Link is Powerful," The National Bureau of Asian Research, October 30, 2023, http://www.nbr.org/publication/india-and-the-quad-when-a-weak-link-is-powerful/.

Sutton, H.I., "China deployed 12 underwater drones in the Indian Ocean," *Forbes*, March 22, 2020, https://www.forbes.com/sites/hisutton/2020/03/22/china-deployed-underwater-drones-in-indian-ocean/#75c4969c6693.

Szechenyi, Nicholas, ed., "China's Maritime Silk Road: Strategic and Economic Implications for the Indo Pacific," Center for Strategic and International Studies, March 2018.

Takakusu, Junjiro, "An introduction to I-tsing's Record of Buddhist religion as practised in India and the Malay Archipelago (AD 671–695)" (PhD diss., Oxford University, 1896), https://jscholarship.library.jhu.edu/bitstream/handle/1774.2/36242/31151010016214.pdf

Tellis, Ashley J., "Hustling in the Himalayas: The Sino-Indian border confrontation," Carnegie Endowment for International Peace, June 4, 2020, https://carnegieendowment.org/2020/06/04/hustling-in-himalayas-sino-indian-border-confrontation-pub-81979.

Till, Geoffrey, "The growing strategic significance of islands," *RSIS Commentary*, November 4, 2019, https://www.rsis.edu.sg/rsis-publication/rsis/the-growing-strategic-significance-of-islands/.

"Today in energy," US Energy Information Administration, December 27, 2019, https://www.eia.gov/todayinenergy/detail.php?id=42338.

USAID, "How a unique trilateral partnership is brining stronger internet to Palau," *Medium*, May 23, 2022, https://medium.com/usaid-invest/how-a-unique-trilateral-partnership-is-bringing-stronger-internet-to-palau-528712045487.

Vego, Milan, "Sea control and sea denial," in *Naval Strategy and Operation in Narrow Seas* (London: Routledge, 1999).

Vego, Milan, "Strategic framework," in *Maritime Strategy and Seas Control: Theory and Practice* (New York: Routledge, 2016).

Venkatanarayanan, S., "Protect indigenous people," *The Hindu*, November 29, 2018, https://www.thehindu.com/opinion/op-ed/protect-indigenous-people/article25616520.ece.

Voyer, Michelle, Genevieve Quirk, Alistar McIlgorm, and Kamal Azmi, "Shades of blue: What do competing interpretations of the blue economy mean for oceans governance?," *Journal of Environmental Policy & Planning* 20, no. 5 (2018): 595–616, https://doi.org/10.1080/1523908X.2018.1473153.

"What's behind the India–China border stand-off?" *BBC News*, July 5, 2017, https://www.bbc.com/news/world-asia-40478813.

White, Joshua T., "China's Indian Ocean ambition: Investment, influence, and military advantage," Brookings Institution, June 2020, https://www.brookings.edu/research/chinas-indian-ocean-ambitions/.

"Why the Suez Canal," Suez Canal Authority, 2019, https://www.suezcanal.gov.eg/English/About/Pages/WhySuezCanal.aspx.

BIBLIOGRAPHY

"The World Factbook," CIA, 2020, https://www.cia.gov/the-world-factbook/.

"World oil transit chokepoints," US Energy Information Administration, July 25, 2017, https://www.eia.gov/international/analysis/special-topics/World_Oil_Transit_Chokepoints.

World Wildlife Fund Report, *Unregulated Fishing on the High Seas of the Indian Ocean: The Impact on, Risk to, and Challenges for Sustainable Fishing and Ocean Health* (Brussels: WWF, 2020), https://wwfeu.awsassets.panda.org/downloads/wwftmt_unregulated_fishing_on_the_high_seas_of_the_indian_ocean_2020.pdf.

Wuwung, Lucky, et al., "Global blue economy governance—A methodological approach to investigating blue economy implementation," *Frontiers in Marine Science* 9 (2022), https://doi.org/10.3389/fmars.2022.1043881.

You Ji, "Dealing with the Malacca dilemma: China's efforts to protect its energy supply," *Strategic Analysis* 31, no. 3 (2007): 467–489.

Zhou Bo, International Maritime Security Conference, May 2023, https://www.rsis.edu.sg/research/idss/research-programmes/maritime-security-programme/imsc/.

Index

Entries for maps, figures, and tables are in *italics*.